TIMEF

HORSES TO

2012/13 JUMPS SEASON

CONTENTS

TIMEFORM

Timeform Horses To Follow is published by Portway Press Ltd, Halifax, West Yorkshire HX1 1XF (Tel: 01422 330330 Fax: 01422 398017; e-mail: timeform@timeform.com).

ISBN 978 1 901570 87 8 Price £8.95

Printed and bound by
Charlesworth Press,
Wakefield, UK 01924 204830

Timeform's Fifty To Follow, carefully chosen by members of Timeform's editorial staff, are listed below with their respective page numbers. A selection of ten (**marked in bold with a ★**) is made for those who prefer a smaller list.

The form summary for each horse is shown after its age, colour, sex and pedigree. The summary shows the distance, the state of the going and where the horse finished in each of its races since the start of the 2011/12 season. Performances are in chronological sequence with the date of its last race shown at the end.

The distance of each race is given in furlongs. Steeplechase form figures are prefixed by the letter 'c' and NH Flat race or bumper form figures by the letter 'F', the others relating to form over hurdles.

The going is symbolised as follows: f=firm, m=good to firm, g=good, d=good to soft, s=soft, v=heavy.

Placings are indicated, up to the sixth place, by use of superior figures, an asterisk being used to denote a win; and superior letters are used to convey what happened to a horse during the race: F-fell, pu-pulled up, ur-unseated rider, bd-brought down, su-slipped up, ro-ran out.

The Timeform Rating of a horse is simply the merit of the horse expressed in pounds and is arrived at by careful examination of its running against other horses. The ratings range from 175+ for the champions down to a figure of around 55 for the meanest selling platers. Symbols attached to the ratings: 'p'–likely to improve; 'P'–capable of much better form; '+' –the horse may be better than we have rated it.

Balder Succes (Fr) h141p

4 b.g Goldneyev (USA) – Frija Eria (Fr) (Kadalko (Fr))
2011/12 18d* 16v* 16d* 16d* 17g^{F} 16v^{ur} Apr 28

Alan King could hardly have been more fulsome in his praise of Balder Succes last season—'I've loved him from day one and he continually impresses me'—and while the gelding did let down his trainer on his last two starts, he remains a smart prospect and looks sure to win a good race or two in 2012/13.

Balder Succes was unbeaten in his four completed outings over hurdles, the first of which came in a newcomers race at Auteuil in October when in the care of Philippe Peltier. After joining King, Balder Success went on to land the odds in a novice at Plumpton and a three-runner juvenile at Ascot, both in January; and he then showed further improvement when accounting for some other promising sorts in a novice on the latter course in February, quickening impressively before two out in winning by seven lengths from Captain Sunshine, whom we have also nominated as one to follow this season. It was a performance which had King comparing Balder Succes favourably with Grumeti, who ended up as the season's top juvenile, when discussing

Balder Succes looks one to follow in his second season over hurdles

their Triumph Hurdle prospects—'We are extremely lucky to have two very good four-year-olds for the race. They would be right up with the best four-year-olds I have had.' Such statements aren't exactly King's stock-in-trade so it was no surprise to see Balder Succes, who unlike many Triumph horses had never run on the Flat, go off at odds of just 15/2 behind his stablemate, the race's market leader. Unfortunately Balder Succes got no further than the fourth, while six weeks later he unseated his rider at the first when 9/4 favourite for the Champion Four Year Old Hurdle at Punchestown. Balder Succes' jumping will improve with experience, though, and with plenty of scope for physical improvement—he's rather unfurnished at present—he should take his form to a still-higher level this term. ***Alan King***

Barlow (Ire) h124+

5 b.g Beneficial – Carrigeen Kerria (Ire) (Kemal (Fr))
2011/12 24v^3 19d* 24s^3 Apr 18

The character of Ken Barlow has been an ever present in the hit soap opera Coronation Street since the first episode back in December 1960, making the man who plays him, William Roache, the world's longest-serving television actor in a continuous role. The horse of that name, on the other hand, is only just starting out on his career, but from what we have seen of him so far it looks as if it could also be a successful one. And hopefully a long one, too!

A point winner in Ireland, and with a fair bit to recommend him on pedigree—he's a brother to the fairly useful bumper winner Carrigeen King and a half-brother to a pair of useful chasers—Barlow fetched £50,000 at the Ascot November Sales and wasted little time in making his presence felt on the track. A promising third in a maiden hurdle at Chepstow on his debut was swiftly followed by a win in a novice at Lingfield in February, in which he and Mr Hopper pulled well clear of the remainder. A defeat on his handicap bow at Cheltenham two months later did little to dent Barlow's promise: the race has the look of strong form for starters, featuring plenty of potential improvers, and Barlow arguably did too much too soon in pressing on three out, eventually finishing third behind Abnaki. Given his pedigree, the three-mile trip shouldn't prove a problem for Barlow another day, whilst the way he travelled for much of the race suggests he's yet to reach his limit as a hurdler, making him a very interesting one for handicaps in the new season, though connections may also have their eyes on a novice chase campaign. Either way, he's one to follow. ***Warren Greatrex***

Big Society (Ire) F109

6 b.g Flemensfirth (USA) – Choice of Kings (Ire) (King's Ride)
2011/12 F17s* F16d^4 Apr 14

Unlike the government's policy of the same name, Big Society came in for plenty of support when he made his debut in a bumper for conditional and amateur riders at Hereford in March, sent off favourite at 9/4 in a nine-runner field made up mostly of newcomers. Despite displaying clear signs of inexperience, tending to race in snatches, Big Society eventually realised what was required and managed to justify that support, getting up near the finish to beat second favourite Young Hurricane.

Big Society, once again ridden by the yard's 7-lb claimer Gerald Quinn, bettered that form under a penalty on his only subsequent start, when finishing three lengths fourth of fourteen to Twelve Roses (also amongst our *Fifty*) in a useful contest at Chepstow, coming out the best horse at the weights on the day and looking one with still more to offer when he goes over hurdles. The manner in which Big Society stayed on close home in both of those races points to him really coming into his own when given the opportunity to tackle distances of two and a half miles and more, something backed up by his stamina-laden pedigree; Big Society is by a strong influence for stamina in Flemensfirth, sire of Imperial Commander and Tidal Bay, and is out of a mare who was a fair hurdler at up to three miles. ***Tom George***

Black Thunder (Fr) ★ h138p

5 bl.g Malinas (Ger) – Blackmika (Fr) (Subotica (Fr))
2011/12 F17m* 16s² 19d* 16s* Apr 9

Whilst Black Thunder is relatively rare in being officially recognised as black, rather than the usual brown, his colour most probably wasn't something which would have persuaded Paul Nicholls to purchase the then untried three-year-old for £30,000 at Doncaster's Spring Sales in 2010. What almost certainly would have influenced Nicholls was the fact that the gelding was from the family of Tataniano, who just over a month earlier had won the Grade 1 Maghull Novices' Chase at Aintree for the trainer.

Around a year after his sale Black Thunder won a bumper at Newton Abbot on his second outing; and he then went on to show useful form in three novice hurdles, winning at Taunton (from Captain Sunshine) and Chepstow. In the latter Black Thunder beat another progressive sort in Princely Player by two and a half lengths, travelling easily into contention and just shaken up to lead between the last two, tending to idle if anything as he and the runner-up pulled well clear of the remainder. Handicaps will come his way if kept to hurdling, but the good-topped Black Thunder is very much a chaser in the making and, of a similar standard to Tataniano at the same stage of their careers, there is no reason why he can't go on and prove just as successful as that one in his first season over fences. Black Thunder, who acts on soft going and won his bumper on good to firm, will stay further than nineteen furlongs. ***Paul Nicholls***

Broadbackbob (IRE) h139p

7 b.g Broadway Flyer (USA) – Back Home (Ire) (Bob Back (USA))
2011/12 16g* 19s* 20d² Jan 28

Anthony Speelman, who can list completing the London Marathon at the age of sixty-five as one of his achievements, has already enjoyed plenty of success as an owner and the exciting Broadbackbob, his sole representative over jumps last season, should provide him with some more good days in 2012/13.

A useful bumper performer when trained in Ireland by Stuart Crawford, Broadbackbob, having been purchased for 80,000 guineas, made an immediate impression on his first start for new connections, beating subsequent Supreme Novices' winner Cinders And Ashes by a length in a minor event at Ascot in November on his hurdling debut. A month later Broadbackbob defied a penalty with a ready defeat of next-time-out winner Ballygarvey in a novice at Newbury, and further improvement followed in defeat, finding the concession of 7 lb to the useful Batonnier just beyond him in a Grade 2 novice at Cheltenham at the end of January. It transpired that Broadbackbob had hurt himself during the race at Prestbury Park, and the injury resulted in his missing the remainder of the season. Although likely to make up into a smart performer if kept to hurdling, Broadbackbob is rising eight and will almost certainly be switched to chasing before too long, and, a good-topped individual, he looks sure to do very well in that sphere. Broadbackbob, who will stay beyond two and a half miles, acts on soft going. ***Nicky Henderson***

Buck Magic (Ire) h119

6 b.g Albano (Ire) – Green Sea (Groom Dancer (USA))
2011/12 22s^3 24d^4 :: 2012/13 23d^6 May 8

Keiran Burke, who struck up a successful partnership with Grade 2-winning hurdler Sparky May in his riding days, turned his attentions to training in 2011, taking over from Sparky May's handler Pat Rodford. In what proved a remarkable first season in his new career, Burke was responsible for Hunt Ball, who made staggering progress and gained the last of seven wins in the Pulteney Land Investments Novices' Handicap, meaning that Burke, who won the 2011 Byrne Group Plate on Holmwood Legend, had achieved the feat of riding and training a winner at successive Cheltenham Festivals.

Burke didn't manage to pick up a race with Buck Magic, but it's only a matter of time before he does. The winner of a maiden point in Ireland in 2010, Buck Magic was successful in a bumper at Taunton and a novice hurdle at Wincanton for Rodford in 2010/11; and he acquitted himself well on the first two of three starts in handicaps for his new handler, particularly first time up when third to subsequent Grade 1 winner Lovcen in a 0-135 event at Wincanton, catching the eye with how he travelled in a race where the form proved to be strong. Landing a race at the Cheltenham Festival is likely to prove beyond Buck Magic, but he's well up to winning handicaps at a lower level. Look out for him if he's sent over fences, too—a tall gelding, he certainly has the physique to make a chaser. Buck Magic stays three miles and acts on soft ground (unraced on firmer than good). ***Keiran Burke***

Dan Barber, Jumps Editor (Buck Magic): *"He'll do well to emulate the progress made last season by Hunt Ball, but Buck Magic can do something to step out of his stablemate's shadow in 2012/13. Buck Magic looked well ahead of his mark in a competitive handicap at Wincanton first time out last term and, still only five, can be forgiven his failure to build immediately on that promise in two subsequent starts."*

In what looks a strong team of novice chasers at Seven Barrows, Captain Conan appeals as one of their best prospects

Captain Conan (Fr) h141

5 b.g Kingsalsa (USA) – Lavandou (Sadler's Wells (USA))

2011/12 17s^3 17s^4 18s* 16s* 18d^6 18d^2 16d^2 Apr 13

Triermore Stud, which can boast Paco Boy among the yearlings it has consigned to the sales, has also started to make its mark on the ownership front, and in 2010 Sent From Heaven carried their pink and royal blue silks into fourth place in the 1000 Guineas. Those colours also came to the fore on the National Hunt scene last season thanks to their first jumper, Captain Conan, who is named after a novel and film which tells the story of a ruthless World War One infantry officer.

The winner of a four-year-old hurdle at Auteuil when trained in France by Antoine Lamotte d'Argy, Captain Conan made a big impression on his British debut in early-January when beating Colour Squadron, who veered left on the run-in, by a short head in Sandown's Tolworth Hurdle, showing his battling qualities. Presumably amiss next time, Captain Conan reproduced his Sandown form on his last two starts when runner-up in Grade 2 novices at Kelso and Aintree, going down by two lengths to Tap Night in the former and by three and three quarter lengths to stablemate Darlan in the latter. Another Henderson-trained runner Oscara Dara (also included in the

Fifty) finished fourth at Aintree, and he went on to boost the form when taking a novice hurdle at Punchestown. Captain Conan, who stays two and a quarter miles and acts on soft ground, is a big, lengthy gelding, very much the type to make an even better chaser, and he could well take high rank in the two-mile novice division. ***Nicky Henderson***

Captain Sunshine h139p

6 b.g Oscar (Ire) – Gaye Fame (Ardross)
2011/12 19d² 21gᶠ 16d² 21d* 20d* Apr 18

Whether or not Captain Sunshine is named after the Neil Diamond song of the early-1970s or the flying cartoon superhero with the ability to produce powerful bursts of solar light we can't say. What we do know is that he is a progressive hurdler who looks sure to win more races when he goes into handicap company.

A promising third on his only start in bumpers in 2010/11, Captain Sunshine raced only in novice hurdles last season and would probably have opened his account but for falling at the last at Kempton on his second outing in January. He made amends in a weaker contest at the same course in March, and the following month gave a performance which cemented his place in this publication when accounting for a field at Cheltenham which included four useful previous winners. Captain Sunshine's jumping still left something to be desired, but he did well to recover from a mistake two out when the race was developing, getting up close home to win by a length from Bold Chief. Sure to become more fluent as he gains further experience and with the scope to improve physically—he's unfurnished at present—Captain Sunshine should continue on the up and, from an opening BHA mark of 134, looks well capable of winning a good handicap this season. As a half-brother to the Irish Grand National winner Oulart and from the family of smart staying chaser Simon, there is every likelihood that Captain Sunshine, who has raced only on good and good to soft ground so far, will prove suited by a step up to three miles. ***Emma Lavelle***

Chesil Beach Boy h132

9 b.g Commanche Run – Eatons (Daring March)
2011/12 21s 20v⁴ 16s* 16s* 16d* 16d⁵ Mar 10

Weymouth's Chesil Beach is one of three major shingle structures in Britain and situated no more than a pebble's throw from the lagoon-side training establishment of John Coombe, whose star performer Chesil Beach Boy did him proud last season and could well do so again this term.

The lightly-raced Chesil Beach Boy showed vastly improved form when dropped back to two miles and switched to handicaps, completing a hat-trick of wins at Wincanton around the turn of the year. On each occasion he was ridden by Coombe's amateur rider daughter Miranda Roberts. The first two of those wins came in novice events, while the last was in open company and saw Chesil Beach Boy show useful form in beating Minella Special by two and a quarter lengths, idling in front and value for more. With Roberts on board once again, Chesil Beach Boy acquitted himself well on his final start when fifth of twenty-four to Paintball in Sandown's Imperial Cup. The usual hold-up tactics were employed but they didn't show Chesil Beach Boy to best advantage on the day, and there may still be better to come from him. The likeable Chesil Beach Boy certainly has the scope to win more races over the smaller obstacles, but it would be no surprise were he to prove a force in novice events should his attentions be turned to chasing in 2012/13, particularly so if partnered by a fully-fledged professional. Chesil Beach Boy, a lengthy gelding, acts on soft ground. ***John Coombe***

Crowning Jewel h122+

6 b.g Sulamani (Ire) – Pennys Pride (Ire) (Pips Pride)
2011/12 F17d* 16s^{2} 19s^{3} 20v^{3} 20g* :: 2012/13 22s^{3} 22m* May 27

For Keith Reveley and Crowning Jewel National Hunt racing is very much in their blood. The former the son of retired leading northern trainer Mary and the father of young jockey James, while the latter is out a half-sister to the top-class chaser Direct Route, from the family of high-class hurdler/smart chaser Youlneverwalkalone. We think it's highly likely that as a combination both can uphold their respective family's good name in 2012/13.

Unlike some of his illustrious relatives Crowning Jewel probably isn't going to be operating at racing's top table any time soon, but that does not preclude him from being a source of profit in handicaps, especially in the North. A bumper and novice hurdle winner in 2011/12 (and placed on his other three starts), the angular gelding was by no means seen to best effect when making his handicap debut at Kelso in early-May, going with zest held up and staying on strongly to finish third of eight to Humbie after a mistake at the final flight. Crowning Jewel followed that effort with a hard-fought victory in a novice hurdle at the same course around three weeks later, once again staying on strongly. The feeling is that Crowning Jewel has yet to show his full hand over timber and, relatively lightly raced, he can achieve plenty more this season from a favourable looking handicap mark (122). Crowning Jewel is likely to stay three miles and acts on soft and good to firm going. ***Keith Reveley***

Decimus (Ire) h105p

5 b.g Bienamado (USA) – Catch Me Dreaming (Ire) (Safety Catch (USA))
2011/12 F17g* F16g 21d 20s :: 2012/13 17d³ May 8

As the third foal and first runner of a poor maiden hurdler, the debutant Decimus wouldn't have made much appeal for those looking at pedigrees to provide a pointer to finding the winner of the maiden bumper at the first of Taunton's November meetings. Decimus did have plenty to recommend him otherwise, though, coming from a stable which was in cracking form at the time and, as a lengthy, useful-looking individual, very much taking the eye in the preliminaries. Decimus also went on to take the eye in the race itself, travelling well before responding generously for pressure to collar another newcomer, the Paul Nicholls-trained Opening Batsman, near the finish.

Opening Batsman went on to show fairly useful form over hurdles in 2011/12, winning two novice events, but the remainder of the season could only be described as disappointing where Decimus was concerned, the gelding finishing down the field in another bumper and two races over hurdles. At that stage there was no way Decimus could have been put forward as one to follow, but there was a good deal more encouragement to take from his performance in a maiden hurdle at Exeter in May. Jumping better than previously, Decimus wasn't knocked about in finishing third of ten behind useful performers Bold Henry and Kian's Delight, looking one who will be fulfilling that debut promise before long, especially if moving into handicaps. Decimus, who should stay two and a half miles, will make a chaser in time, but there are races to be won with him over hurdles first. ***Jeremy Scott***

Double Ross (Ire) h131

6 ch.g Double Eclipse (Ire) – Kinross (Nearly A Hand)
2011/12 19d³ 16g⁵ 17v* 21s³ 16v² 16g 21g 22d² :: 2012/13 16d³ May 12

A glance at his pedigree is enough to deduce how Double Ross came to be named; while it is also an indication that he is bred more for stamina than speed and speaks volumes for his performance in the two-mile Swinton Hurdle at Haydock when last seen in May. Double Ross finished third of nineteen to Red Merlin in that well-contested handicap, making the running, jumping well apart from a mistake two out and finding plenty for pressure. He'll be worth noting when returned to further over hurdles, while in the longer term the strongly-made Double Ross, a brother to the useful chaser Mr Moonshine, will prove at least as effective over fences.

Double Ross's only win to date came in a novice event at Folkestone, but he subsequently ran well to be placed on three occasions prior to the Swinton, finishing third to Fingal Bay in the Challow Novices' at Newbury, two and a half lengths second to subsequent Supreme Novices' winner Cinders And Ashes in the three-runner Rossington Main Novices' at Haydock and second of fourteen to Sainglend in a novice at Stratford. The last-named event was run over two and three quarter miles, and while Double Ross could exploit his current mark of 130 over two miles given a thorough test, it is at two and a half miles and more that we expect him to shine. Double Ross has run his best races on ground softer than good, with his sole success coming on heavy. ***Nigel Twiston-Davies***

Dreambrook Lady (Ire) h124

6 b.m Alderbrook – Easter Day (Ire) (Simply Great (Fr))

2011/12 F17g 16g^6 17g^4 17v^4 16s* 16v^F 16s* 16g^5 16g^4 17s^3 :: 2012/13 16d^{pu} May 12

I think we can safely assume that either Ms Mary Miles owns a company that sells mattresses or very much keeps her fingers crossed when naming her racehorses. Our Little Dreamer, Honourable Dreamer, Dream Catcher, Dream Cloud and Josh's Dreamway have all worn the owner's red and emerald green silks in recent seasons, and we're confident Dreambrook Lady can give all concerned plenty of days to get out of bed for in 2012/13.

Dreambrook Lady on the way to the latter of her wins last season

Down the field in a bumper on her debut, Dreambrook Lady improved by the run over hurdles, showing promise in three novices before justifying favouritism in a mares' novice event at Huntingdon on her handicap debut (mark of 87) in mid-January. Following an unfortunate final-flight departure at Chepstow, Dreambrook Lady quickly regained the winning thread when taking another handicap at Huntingdon, this time off 102, in February. In form terms better was to follow, though, with Dreambrook Lady's fourth to Laudatory in a similar event at Stratford in March and third behind Une Artiste and Swincombe Flame in a mares' novices' listed race at Cheltenham in April both fairly useful performances. Her most recent effort, pulled up in the Swinton at Haydock, is easily excused as it came after she'd been on the go for a long time.

From a still underrated yard and hailing from the family of top-class chaser Simply Dashing, the patiently-ridden Dreambrook Lady is still unexposed beyond two miles. A rangy mare, she appeals as the type to make a better chaser and is one to watch out for over fences, especially when the ground is on the soft side (acts on heavy).
Jeremy Scott

Dynaste (Fr) h158

6 gr.g Martaline – Bellissima de Mai (Fr) (Pistolet Bleu (Ire))
2011/12 24d* 25s^4 24d^2 24g Mar 15

A cursory glance at the train timetables indicates that the trip from Worcester to Cheltenham can be made in a rather brisk twenty-nine minutes. Although taking slightly longer than that, Dynaste made his own journey from a Worcester novice to the World Hurdle at the Festival in relatively quick time, and we expect him to make to make similar strides over fences in the upcoming season.

Quickly putting a rather inauspicious start to his British career at Worcester behind him, David Pipe's grey progressed through the handicap ranks, his stint in that sphere culminating in a wide-margin demolition of a competitive field at Haydock last November, sparking comparisons with the stable's previous winner of the race Grands Crus. Dynaste's three subsequent runs last term all came in graded company, finishing behind the dominant Big Buck's on each occasion, and he advanced his own form when seven lengths second to Paul Nicholls' superstar in the Cleeve Hurdle at Cheltenham in January. Dynaste failed to repeat that performance at the Festival on his final outing, when tongue tied for the first time and also ridden with restraint (usually makes the running).

Following a similar path to the aforementioned Grands Crus, it now appears that Dynaste is going to attempt to make his mark in staying novice chases, and the style in which he devoured the Fixed Brush hurdles at Haydock allied to the very smart form

Dynaste jumping Haydock's Fixed Brush hurdles with aplomb, which bodes well for his prospects over fences

he has shown over timber bodes extremely well for Dynaste's chances of making the grade over fences. A lengthy sort with the physique for chasing, Dynaste stays three miles and acts on soft ground. ***David Pipe***

Eleven Fifty Nine F110

6 b.m Midnight Legend – Essex Bird (Primitive Rising (USA))
2011/12 F16d² F16v² F16d³ F17d* Apr 13

While it may only be through coincidence that she shares her name with a song by popular New York band Blondie, Eleven Fifty Nine is proving not too dissimilar to the group's iconic singer Debbie Harry in making her presence well and truly known in what is traditionally a male-dominated environment. The good-bodied mare, rapidly becoming impressive young trainer Anthony Honeyball's number one prospect, can certainly enjoy more days in the sun this season.

Despite having a pedigree that hardly inspired (first foal out of a limited mare), Eleven Fifty Nine was only a 7/1 shot when making her debut in a thirteen-runner bumper at Worcester in the summer of 2010 and duly won with a degree of comfort, despite needing strong driving to get the message once asked. Given a break of four months, Eleven Fifty Nine had her first start of last season in a similar race at Chepstow and, while in form terms it wasn't much of an improvement on her opening effort, subsequent events proved she faced a stiff task up against the Philip Hobbs-trained Colour Squadron. Better was to follow when Eleven Fifty Nine again reached the frame on her next two outings, looking the part and better than the result (asked to make a lot of ground in the straight) when not beaten far by Call Me Star and Umadachar in a listed race at Sandown on the latter occasion. Again ridden by Honeyball's partner and assistant trainer Rachael Green (as she has been for all her runs), Eleven Fifty Nine progressed that little bit further to reverse form with the same two horses in another listed contest at Aintree's Grand National meeting on her final start, overcoming her edginess in the preliminaries once more and ideally suited by the flatter track. That success provided the yard with its most notable winner to date, too.

While acknowledging that the plan is reportedly for Eleven Fifty Nine to tackle mares' novice hurdles this term with races such as the David Nicholson at the Cheltenham Festival on the long-term agenda, her trainer's record in handicap hurdles—25% strike rate for a £37.03 level-stakes profit (to a £1 stake) over the past five seasons—means it would clearly be worth taking heed were she to crop up in such a race during the campaign. Eleven Fifty Nine has shown her form on both heavy and good to firm ground. ***Anthony Honeyball***

Fourth Estate (Ire) h124p

6 b.g Fantastic Light (USA) – Papering (Ire) (Shaadi (USA))
2011/12 17s* 16g* 20g^{4} Apr 7

Despite a record of four wins from five career starts, it's probably fair to say Fourth Estate has been brought along fairly quietly and without much fanfare so far, largely kept away from the major meetings, but we fancy him to make some bigger headlines for himself in 2012/13.

Fourth Estate fetched only £4,500 as a two-year-old the only time he has ever been through a sales ring, but his pedigree is hardly undistinguished, with his dam second in the Nassau, Yorkshire Oaks and Prix Vermeille as a three-year-old and also responsible for useful winners under both codes, and he put his inherent Flat speed to good use when winning both of his starts in bumpers. Consequently an odds-on shot when making his hurdling debut in a Folkestone novice in January, Fourth Estate's performance in beating Avoca Promise (won subsequently) appeared only workmanlike but better was to come when he followed up in a similar event at Doncaster just over a month later, beating runaway Lingfield winner Netherby by a length, jumping soundly and displaying a likeable attitude. While Fourth Estate managed only fourth to Grandads Horse in a Haydock Fixed Brush novice event on his handicap debut, he seemed to fail for stamina over two and a half miles having loomed up and looked the likeliest winner two out. Raced only on good or softer ground so far, Fourth Estate can regain the winning thread at around two miles whether it be in handicaps over timber (his mark of 123 remains unchanged) or in novice chases. ***Nicky Henderson***

Gevrey Chambertin (Fr) ★ F108

4 gr.g Dom Alco (Fr) – Fee Magic (Fr) (Phantom Breeze)
2011/12 F16v* F16g^{4} Feb 17

Early in the 1980s there were Gaye Brief and Gaye Chance; and since then we have had Morley Street and Granville Again, Cyborgo and Hors La Loi III, Best Mate and Cornish Rebel and Denman and Silverburn. So, what are the chances of Grands Crus and Gevrey Chambertin being the next set of full brothers to both succeed at Grade 1 level? We think it could well happen. Grands Crus has played his part already by winning the Feltham Novices' Chase last year, while the promise shown by Gevrey Chambertin in his two starts in bumpers points to his making a big impact when he goes jumping.

Gevrey Chambertin, named after an area known for its Grand Cru Burgundy, looked well above average first time up, winning a newcomers bumper at Ffos Las in December by thirty lengths. Two months later, under much less testing conditions, he ran to a similar level of form in a far stronger contest, a listed race no less, at Newbury. Having forced the pace, Gevrey Chambertin was held in third when squeezed out in the final furlong and finished fourth behind the unbeaten Shutthefrontdoor, beaten less than five lengths. There's plenty of stamina in Gevrey Chambertin's pedigree and he shapes as if he's going to prove a stronger stayer than Grands Crus, so a step up to two and half miles and more will serve him well in his first season over hurdles, when he will pay to follow. ***David Pipe***

Gotoyourplay (Ire) h102 c127p

8 ch.g Definite Article – Johnston's Flyer (Ire) (Orchestra)
2011/12 21d^{4} c22s* c23g^{F} c24d* Mar 6

Although an eight-year-old, Gotoyourplay is still very much unexposed, with his career under Rules spanning only five starts so far (across two seasons), and we think it's a fair bet that he'll have more to offer in the upcoming season. A point winner, Gotoyourplay fetched £25,000 at the sales in January 2011, and had his first taste of racing under Rules just over a month later. A modest fourth in a maiden chase at Taunton first time up, Gotoyourplay was again sympathetically handled when filling the same position in a novice hurdle at Towcester nine months later. Only sixteen days on from his return to the track, Gotoyourplay proved emphatically that the education was not lost on him when causing a minor shock (although he was backed from 20/1 into 14/1) returned to fences in winning on his handicap bow off a mark of 110 at Newbury.

Gotoyourplay is one to keep on side in staying handicap chases in 2012/13

There's no denying it was disappointing to see Gotoyourplay hit the deck on his next start (chasing the leaders when falling at the eleventh) and, while the remnants of that negative experience may have been the reason for his tendency to make mistakes on his final run in 2011/12, the fact that he still managed to regain the winning thread in a novice at Exeter bodes very well indeed.

There's little doubt that his trainer will have subjected Gotoyourplay to some intense schooling sessions during the off-season and it is worth pointing out that not only is his sire responsible for smart chasers Majestic Concorde, Non So, Fistral Beach and Doeslessthanme, but Gotoyourplay also hails from the family of the useful handicap chaser Mattock Ranger. With that in mind, it's anticipated that Gotoyourplay can prove a fair deal better than his current BHA mark of 125 over the larger obstacles, with marathon distances likely to suit well in due course. ***Andy Turnell***

Grabtheglory (Ire) h121p

6 b.g Accordion – Full of Surprises (Ire) (Be My Native (USA))
2011/12 F18m* 20g^{2} 21g* 19g^{2} 24s^{ur} 24g^{3} Feb 17

With the London Olympics having undoubtedly been the highlight of the summer, the aptly-named Grabtheglory, who hasn't finished outside the bronze medal position in all of his seven completed outings, could well prove one of the stars of the show this winter.

A fairly useful bumper winner, Grabtheglory has always been held in high regard by Gary Moore ('I love this horse') and was given a summer break before reappearing over hurdles in a novice at Fontwell in October. After finding only the now useful Arab League too good that day, Stanley J Cohen's tall and scopey gelding quickly opened his account over timber when narrowly beating Twentyfourcarat in a similar race at Kempton. Grabtheglory then went on to produce good efforts either side of an unfortunate blip at Ascot, particularly catching the eye when third behind the prolific Knock A Hand and Gullinbursti, in a Newbury handicap off a BHA mark of 120, off the bridle much later than those two rivals but simply failing for stamina over the three-mile trip. The brother to fairly useful hurdler Gus Macrae , from the family of Buck House and Jessies Dream, was then due to run in a valuable handicap hurdle for novices at Sandown in March but unfortunately scoped dirty in the lead up to the race. Given plenty of time to recover by a much respected yard, it would be no surprise if Grabtheglory soon established himself as useful in 2012/13, when he will pay to follow in handicaps. Often a strong traveller, Grabtheglory will prove best short of three miles and acts on good to soft ground (bumper win on good to firm). ***Gary Moore***

Gullinbursti (Ire) h140

6 b.g Milan – D'Ygrande (Ire) (Good Thyne (USA))
2011/12 21s* 22s* 24g^{2} 24g^{2} 24d Apr 13

The black and pink check cap silks of owner Nick Mustoe, the Managing Director of a marketing and advertising agency who apparently got into horses after a trainer said that if he learned to ride he would let him have a go on a racehorse, have become a familiar sight in the winners enclosure in recent years thanks to the likes of Kangaroo Court, Court In Motion and Benign Dictator. Gullinbursti, whose name translates as 'Gold Mane' or 'Golden Bristles' and is the moniker of a boar in Norse mythology, added to Mustoe's tally in the latest season with two wins over timber, which bodes very well for what this prospective chaser will achieve over the larger obstacles this term.

The first foal of a bumper/two-and-a-half-mile chase winner and purchased for 28,000 guineas as a three-year-old, Gullinbursti was a fairly useful bumper winner himself for Peter Colville in Ireland during the 2010/11 season, and he quickly proved better than that for his current trainer when winning novice hurdles at Exeter and Hereford (three of next four finishers won next time) in November. Gullinbursti then proved three miles holds no fears for him by finishing three and three quarter lengths second behind Rocky Creek (another of our *Fifty*) in the Grade 2 River Don Novices' Hurdle at Doncaster in January, an effort made even more meritorious when it was reported that he'd missed a week's work having pulled off a shoe and stepped on a nail in the lead up to the race. In form terms, Gullinbursti only matched that level when a neck second to Knock A Hand on his handicap debut at Newbury less than a month later, but it was still a run that confirmed he was a horse going places, just failing. Having bypassed the Cheltenham Festival owing to his trainer's going concerns—'he needs genuine soft ground to be seen at his best'—Gullinbursti's low-key final outing in the Sefton Novice's Hurdle at Aintree is easily forgiven, with the horse shaping as if amiss. A big and lengthy sort who quickly reached a useful level over hurdles, Gullinbursti has all the hallmarks of one who will do even better over the larger obstacles and he could prove a major force in novice chases in 2012/13. ***Emma Lavelle***

Gurtacrue (Ire) c123p

7 ch.g Deploy – Biddy Early (Ire) (Sharp Charter)
2011/12 c24d[5] c28d[3] c25d* c25g Mar 15

Being heavily involved in the point-to-point scene, it is little surprise that owners William and Angela Rucker appear to have a penchant for staying chasers, with State of Play, Cappa Bleu and High Chimes having all carried their royal blue and pink colours to great success during the last decade. The latest representative we expect to provide the Worcestershire-based couple with plenty to celebrate is the unexposed Gurtacrue.

Successful in two points and a bumper in Ireland prior to being bought for £95,000 at the Doncaster Sales in August 2010, Gurtacrue won a maiden hurdle in his first season with Evan Williams, but he'd always looked a chaser in the making and the switch to fences last term brought about immediate improvement. Fifth to Ace High in what turned out to be a strong beginners' chase at Chepstow first time up, Gurtacrue got off the mark over the larger obstacles two starts later in a novice handicap at Wincanton in January, shaping even better than the result in beating Minella Stars a neck having idled a shade after taking over early in the straight. Gurtacrue faced a much stiffer test on his only subsequent start, in the Kim Muir at Cheltenham, but he acquitted himself well in finishing eighth of twenty-three behind Sunnyhillboy in that valuable amateurs handicap, going well for a long way and shaping as though a mark 5 lb higher than at Wincanton underestimates him. Gurtacrue, who acts on soft going, will stay beyond three and a half miles and could make up into a Grand National horse in time, but there are plenty of lesser races to be won with him first. ***Evan Williams***

High Office h95p

6 b.g High Chaparral (Ire) – White House (Pursuit of Love)
2011/12 17v4 16s4 16g Jan 13

To some extent, we've been here before. Trainer Richard Fahey and owner Jim Parsons enjoyed plenty of success with smart Flat performer Vintage Premium in the early stages of this millennium and even gave the John Smith's Cup winner a chance to make his mark over hurdles, the then six-year-old showing plenty of encouragement in a trio of outings during the 2003/4 season. Vintage Premium never got the chance to build on that form, suffering a fatal injury on the gallops, but hopefully the same connections' middle-distance handicapper High Office can win a handicap or two over timber after showing quiet promise in his three qualifying runs last term.

High Office was dropped in at the deep end in more ways than one on his hurdling debut, the rather leggy bay showing promise but ultimately proving no match for future Supreme Novices' winner Cinders And Ashes, smart bumper performer Keys and Ile de Re (another to make our *Fifty*), in a heavy-ground maiden at Aintree. Despite again looking unsuited by testing conditions, High Office showed more in a similar event at Catterick just over three weeks later before catching the eye when seventh in a Musselburgh race in which four of the first six won next time out, spared a hard time. An opening mark of 102 could prove potentially very lenient for High Office bearing in mind his useful form on the level (stays a mile and three quarters and placed three times in handicaps in 2012) and that he has shown some aptitude for hurdling on all three of his runs so far, and it will be disappointing if this consistent sort fails to land handicaps when the ground isn't too gruelling. ***Richard Fahey***

Jamie Lynch, Chief Correspondent (High Office): *"Six is getting on a bit for the Flat, but just getting started over jumps, which is exactly the stage High Office is at in his career. He's inevitably found it harder up against the younger legs on the Flat this season, but still showing the ability and enthusiasm that will get him a long way as a hurdler. Good luck to High Office in his new pursuit, though he doesn't need it, not from a starting handicap mark of 102."*

Horatio Hornblower (Ire) ★ F108

4 b.g Presenting – Countess Camilla (Bob's Return (Ire))
2011/12 F16g^3 F16g Mar 14

Good things come to those who wait according to marketing advisors representing popular brands of tomato ketchup and Irish dry stout, and it's a maxim followed by a number of National Hunt trainers, Nick Williams being one of them. The Devon handler is far from a regular presence in the traditional training ground for future jumpers—National Hunt Flat races—yet it's worth noting that his last two winners in that sphere at the time of writing, Swincombe Flame and Diamond Harry, turned out to be well worth following over obstacles, the latter developing into a high-class, Hennessy-winning chaser.

Unlike his aforementioned stablemates, Horatio Hornblower failed to make a winning debut. Yet the gelding, named after a C.S. Forester-created Royal Navy officer once described as 'admirable' by Sir Winston Churchill, could hardly have shown much more promise in what traditionally is one of the strongest pre-Cheltenham Festival bumpers. The listed event run at Newbury in mid-February attracted a field of twelve, eight of whom were previous winners, and Horatio Hornblower showed useful form in finishing third behind the still-unbeaten Shutthefrontdoor and Village Vic, one place ahead of another of our *Fifty*, Gevrey Chambertin. The strong suspicion is that Horatio Hornblower's subsequent effort, when down the field in the Champion Bumper at Cheltenham, was a result of his having had quite a hard race on his debut and his potential for better remains very much intact. Bred for jumping - his dam, a half-sister to the very smart chaser up to three miles Our Ben, was a fairly useful hurdler up to two and a half miles—the rangy Horatio Hornblower certainly looks the type to excel over obstacles, and he could even end up making waves in some of the good-class novice events over timber this term. ***Nick Williams***

Ifyouletmefinish (Ire) h131

5 b.g Bonbon Rose (Fr) – Surfing France (Fr) (Art Francais (USA))
2011/12 F16m* F16g 17d^3 17d^2 17d* 17g :: 2012/13 16d May 12

Jeremy Scott has not long since switched his full attention to training racehorses having previously spent his mornings milking cows on his Somerset farm, which forms part of the Exmoor National Park. In the summer of 2008, after a successful season, the cows were kindly escorted off the premises to leave Scott free to apply his expertise fully to getting the best out of the likes of Scottish National runner-up Gone To Lunch, Devon National hero Clash Duff and now Ifyouletletmefinish.

Scott's yard hit a rich vein of form towards the end of last October, at which time Ifyouletmefinish made a successful debut in a bumper at Uttoxeter. Switched to hurdling after his next start, Ifyouletmefinish was placed in a couple of strong novices at Taunton before showing useful form when dead-heating with subsequent listed winner Urbain de Sivola in a similar race there in February. Ifyouletmefinish showed up for a long way in the County Hurdle at Cheltenham on his next outing, and on his second run in handicap company he finished a creditable seventh to Red Merlin in Haydock's Swinton Hurdle in May, looking ready for a step up in trip, in line with his pedigree. Whilst the latter performance suggested he still has more to offer over timber from his current mark of 134, there's little doubt Ifyouletmefinish has the makings of a chaser and he's sure to win races over fences in 2012/13 if aimed that way—it's worth noting that Scott's runners in handicaps over the larger obstacles have shown a level-stakes profit during the last five seasons. Ifyouletmefinish, tongue tied apart from when gaining his win over hurdles, acts on good to soft ground but also has a bumper win on good to firm. ***Jeremy Scott***

Ile de Re (Fr) ★ h121+

6 gr.g Linamix (Fr) – Ile Mamou (Ire) (Ela-Mana-Mou)
2011/12 17v^3 19d^2 16s* 16d* 16d Mar 10

Although Ile de Re won the 2011 Shergar Cup Stayers Handicap at Ascot under Japanese superstar Yutaka Take, a rider so famous in his home country that he has lent his name to a video game, his greater claim to fame is that in 2012, on his first two starts for Donald McCain, he completed the Chester Cup/Northumberland Plate double, the first to do so since Attivo in 1974.

McCain has quickly established himself as the premier jumps trainer of the North and has an uncanny ability to conjure improvement out of his new recruits. A particularly relevant example is his handling of Weird Al, a horse who, like Ile de Re, he inherited from the Ian Williams yard. Weird Al was rejuvenated by the Grand National-winning trainer last season, landing the Charlie Hall Chase and finishing third in the Betfair Chase. Ile de Re himself showed fairly useful form for Williams in his first season over hurdles, winning novice events at Huntingdon and Sandown, and his improved efforts on the Flat for McCain since point to his reaching an even higher level this term. Currently rated only 123 over hurdles by the BHA, Ile de Re could make hay in handicaps in the near future, especially as he is still very much unexposed trip-wise; stamina has proved the grey's forte on the Flat, yet apart from when runner-up over nineteen furlongs on his second start he has raced only around two miles over hurdles. Although he has won on good to firm, Ile de Re's best performances on the level have come on soft and heavy ground, so it's no surprise that he's yet to race on going quicker than good to soft over timber. ***Donald McCain***

Jayandbee (Ire) h97p

5 b.g Presenting – Christines Gale (Ire) (Strong Gale)
2011/12 F16d³ F16s 20s⁶ 20d 20d⁴ Apr 22

Philip Hobbs has numerous big races on his CV, including the Champion Hurdle, the Queen Mother Champion Chase and the Guinness Gold Cup, but it seems fair to assume that he also gets a kick out of outwitting the official assessor. The likes of Big Easy, Qaspal and Marchand d'Argent have all been well-supported winners on their handicap debuts over hurdles in recent seasons and we envisage Jayandbee continuing the sequence this term.

Owners the Gibbs family have enjoyed success with the likes of the Hobbs-trained One Knight and Voramar Two in recent seasons and their Jayandbee, a half-brother to the fair hurdler at up to three miles Ben's Turn, showed promise in his two outings in bumpers, his better effort a fair third to subsequent listed winner One Term at Chepstow in October. Having been given a break of four months, Jayandbee was then not knocked about in each of his three runs in maiden/novice hurdles, with easily his best performance coming when fourth to Victor Leudorum (followed up next time) at Wincanton on his final start. That most recent appearance really pointed Jayandbee out as a horse to keep well on side in the near future, with the five-year-old doing well to finish just over a dozen lengths behind the winner despite not being given an overly-hard time by Richard Johnson.

A good-topped sort bred on the same direct cross as high-class chaser Woolcombe Folly and Grade 1-winning novice chaser Another Promise, Jayandbee is very much the type to do better and his opening handicap mark of 105 most probably underestimates him. ***Philip Hobbs***

Kazlian (Fr) h139

4 b.g Sinndar (Ire) – Quiet Splendor (USA) (Unbridled (USA))
2011/12 17g² 16v* 16d* 16g⁴ 16d Apr 14

Let's hope that Tom Scudamore isn't a devotee of Michael Jackson, or else one suspects that he may still have the popular ballad 'Gone Too Soon' playing in his mind following Kazlian's effort at the Cheltenham Festival. Following wins in a juvenile hurdle at Ffos Las and a novice at Leicester, Kazlian was well fancied when making his handicap debut off a mark of 130 in the Fred Winter, and David Pipe's French bred shaped like the best-treated horse in the race despite finishing fourth to Une Artiste, impressing with the way he drew clear on the bridle between four and three out having jumped most fluently towards the head of affairs but undoubtedly asked for his effort far earlier than ideal. The famous Cheltenham hill can be an imposing obstacle at the best of times, but for the weary Kazlian it must have been an especially unwelcome sight. With that in mind, it was hardly surprising to see him turn in a rather lethargic performance at Aintree a month later, when ridden in markedly different fashion.

Being only a four-year-old there is plenty of time for Kazlian to realise his undoubted potential and a current BHA handicap mark of 136 shouldn't represent the peak of his ability. Seemingly uncomplicated in terms of ground preference (though yet to race on firmer than good), Kazlian looks sure to take a leading role in some of the more valuable two-mile handicap hurdles this coming season, with his pedigree (Flat bred and showed useful form in five runs on the level in France) and enthusiastic running style dictating that his immediate future probably lies over the minimum distance. Whilst he may not be flying too far under the radar, Kazlian is still likely to be a profitable horse to follow in 2012/13. ***David Pipe***

Kentford Grey Lady — h136p

6 gr.m Silver Patriarch (Ire) – Kentford Grebe (Teenoso (USA))
2011/12 16g^{5} 19s^{3} 21s* 24g* 24d^{2} 20g^{2} Mar 13

In recent seasons the mares Easter Legend, Labelthou and half-sisters Mayberry and Blaeberry have all done well for Emma Lavelle, and the latest example of girl power at Cottage Stables is Kentford Grey Lady, who has already won three of her eight races for the yard and could yet prove the pick of the bunch.

A fair bumper winner in her debut season, Kentford Grey Lady returned over hurdles in 2011/12 and was soon showing useful form in mares races. Successful in a novice event at Newbury in November and a mares handicap at Kempton the following month, Kentford Grey Lady was runner-up subsequently in a couple of Grade 2 contests. In the Warfield at Ascot she was beaten half a length by Violin Davis, and was then just four lengths behind Quevega in the twenty-runner David Nicholson at Cheltenham, where she finished strongly in a race which wasn't run to suit. All in all, a highly productive season that promised more to come. The likelihood is that Kentford Grey Lady will be kept over timber for another season, but she will also be of plenty of interest if tried over fences. The lengthy Kentford Grey Lady looks the part for chasing, while her dam, a half-sister to useful chaser The Land Agent, was a fair winner over the larger obstacles herself. Kentford Grey Lady, who is usually held up, stays three miles, though she is not short of speed. She acts on soft going. ***Emma Lavelle***

Lie Forrit (Ire) h150 c133p

8 b.g Subtle Power (Ire) – Ben Roseler (Ire) (Beneficial)
2011/12 c22s* c22s[2] c25v[2] Feb 6

Never mind a few hundred words, a whole book could be devoted to Lie Forrit. Purchased for just £4,000 as a foal by his octogenarian part-owner John McNeill, Lie Forrit defied odds of 100/1 when taking a Carlisle bumper on his debut five years ago and has been a star for trainer Willie Amos since—such was the progress he made that he was once asked to take on the mighty Big Buck's in the World Hurdle. The latest chapter in his story undoubtedly centres on the tragic loss of Campbell Gillies, who partnered Lie Forrit in all fifteen of the gelding's races to date and will be greatly missed.

Lie Forrit shrugged off an absence of nearly twenty-one months (had suffered a tendon injury) when making an impressive start over fences in December, landing the odds from Blenheim Brook in a novice race at Kelso. He was then beaten twice in three-runner similar contests, by the same horse at Ayr latterly, following a reverse to another Lucinda Russell runner, the promising Bold Sir Brian, at Kelso. However, there is no doubt that Lie Forrit was unsuited by the steady pace on both occasions and the potential to match his smart hurdles form over the larger obstacles remains. In fact, Lie Forrit, who will stay beyond twenty-five furlongs, could well pick up a good staying handicap. The Scottish National is one race connections of Lie Forrit might have in mind for him, the gelding having had to miss the latest running when contracting flu-like symptoms. He has done all of his racing on ground softer than good. ***Willie Amos***

Simon Walker, Head of Editorial (Lie Forrit): *"He might be knocking on a bit for a horse with only three starts to his name over fences, but this one-time smart hurdler provided more than enough encouragement in that trio of runs last season to think he'll ultimately prove himself as good over fences. And if that does prove to be the case then not only does his initial BHA mark underestimate him but there's a strong chance he'll pick up a good long-distance handicap or two over the winter."*

Lord Wishes (Ire) F111

5 b.g Milan – Strong Wishes (Ire) (Strong Gale)
2011/12 F16v* F16d* Mar 21

A former amateur jockey and also assistant to such as Ferdy Murphy and Guillaume Macaire, James Ewart set up as a trainer as recently as 2004 and since 2007/08 the yard's number of winners per season has increased year-on-year, reaching twenty-three last term. In short, Ewart is a trainer on the up, and in Lord Wishes he has a very exciting prospect who should help his stable achieve even greater success in 2012/13.

Lord Wishes apparently goes by the name of Porsche at home, and those aware of that prior to his debut in a bumper at Ayr in January would probably have considered his price of 2/1 a generous one. In proving as much, Lord Wishes gave an impressive performance, making the running and powering through the heavy ground under mainly hand riding in the final two furlongs, drawing twelve lengths clear. On his only other appearance almost two months later, Lord Wishes gave another taking display when defying a penalty at Haydock, travelling strongly close up before taking control early in the straight. Although tending to idle in front, he still had six lengths to spare over his nearest pursuer No Duffer come the line. Lord Wishes, a tall imposing sort, looks just the sort to take well to hurdling, and that he has reportedly done plenty of work with renowned jumping coach Yogi Breisner is a big plus. He has the potential to prove amongst the top northern novices this season. ***James Ewart***

Makethe Mostofnow (Ire) h133

7 b.g Milan – Pass The Leader (Ire) (Supreme Leader)
2011/12 24d^{4} 20v* 22v^{6} 20v* 24v* 24d^{bd} Apr 13

The finish of the second division of the six-year-old maiden run at Punchestown's point-to-point course on February 13 in 2011 was fought out between two horses who have gone on to show themselves well above average as hurdlers, namely Makethe Mostofnow and Lovcen. The former came out on top, by three lengths, but whereas Lovcen, now with Alan King, was led out unsold at £40,000 at Cheltenham's April Sales just two months later, Makethe Mostofnow was knocked down to Evan Williams for £20,000, around half the price he'd realised at Doncaster as a three-year-old. Makethe Mostofnow already looks a bargain, having won a maiden and two novice events, all at Ffos Las, from five completed starts in his first season over hurdles.

Makethe Mostofnow showed useful form when gaining the last two of those wins, on the latter occasion travelling strongly, leading after two out and going on to score by eight lengths from Miss Kalifa. Whilst the manner of that success suggested Makethe Mostofnow had a bigger performance in him, it was a little surprising to see him fast-tracked to Grade 1 company for his next start, in the Sefton Novices' at Aintree's Grand National meeting. It was a clear indication of the regard in which he's held by connections, but unfortunately Makethe Mostofnow got no further than the fourth, where he was brought down. The race, incidentally, was won by none other than Lovcen. Makethe Mostofnow certainly has the potential to be competitive in handicap hurdles off his opening mark of 139. However, he looks every inch a chaser and we think he will be making a significant impact over fences in 2012/13, with races at around three miles in the mud (all three hurdle wins gained on heavy) likely to prove right up his street. ***Evan Williams***

Marshal Zhukov (Ire) h115

6 b.g Morozov (USA) – Artic Brush (Ire) (Brush Aside (USA))
2011/12 24d^3 21d^4 18s^3 19g^5 18d* Apr 20

Marshal Zhukov, named after the man who would become the most decorated general officer in the history of the Soviet Union and Russia, is unlikely to be making such an indelible mark in jumps racing. He should pick up a medal or two this season, though, be it over hurdles or fences. A runner-up in points prior to showing a little ability in bumpers in 2010/11, Marshal Zhukov opened his account on the last of his five starts over hurdles in 2011/12, in an eight-runner handicap at Fontwell in April. Partnered once again by promising conditional James Best, Marshal Zhukov showed fairly useful form as he produced a vastly improved effort to score by fourteen lengths from Warsaw Pact, travelling much the best from some way out and soon clear after taking over before the second last.

Marshal Zhukov will continue to do well if kept to hurdling, but his trainer has a good record with chasers—in the last five seasons she has had roughly as many winners over fences as over hurdles from approximately half the amount of runners—and it would be no surprise if this lengthy sort finds himself contesting races over the larger obstacles in the near future. Marshal Zhukov is a free-going individual who may prove best at short of three miles, and he acts on good to soft going. ***Caroline Keevil***

Master Malt F112

4 b.g Milan – Mrs Malt (Ire) (Presenting)
2011/12 F16m^2 Apr 21

There's the Moores daan Saarf, the Easterby's up in't North and the Hills family somewhere in the middle. But, away from the madding crowd, in the deepest depths of the Scottish Borders, there's a new dynasty gathering pace, that of the Clan Whillans, who are starting to become a force to be reckoned with in National Hunt racing.

Alistair Whillans, whose brother Donald is also a trainer on the up and father of McCain-based conditional Callum, is responsible for our darkest of dark horses this season, with the once-raced Master Malt one of the most unexposed performers amongst our *Fifty*. Owned by the Distillery Stud, Master Malt made his debut under the trainer's son Ewan (sibling Garry is also a conditional rider) in a bumper at Ayr on Scottish National day in April. The second foal out of an unraced sister to the useful hurdler/chaser at up to two and three quarter miles Cockney Trucker, Master Malt met with some support in the market and showed precisely why in the race itself, running with huge promise at odds of 11/1. Having made eye-catching headway from off the pace to join in on the bridle turning in, Master Malt pulled clear with the more experienced Nicky Henderson-trained winner River Maigue (odds on), giving best only late on, and appealing as the type who should have little trouble shedding his maiden tag in a similar race. While connections have that option open for Master Malt, he also appeals as one to look out for in novice/handicap hurdles, with his trainer already enjoying plenty of success with his runners over timber so far in 2012/13 (28% strike rate at the time of writing).
Alistair Whillans

Module (Fr) h135p

5 b.g Panoramic – Before Royale (Fr) (Dauphin du Bourg (Fr))
2011/12 17s^{5} 18s^{bd} 17d* Jan 28

Tom George's top four earners last season in terms of win prize money were all bred in France, with all bar the last-named of Nacarat, Baby Mix, Module and Sivola de Sivola having begun their racing career in their native country also. The likely key to George's Gallic affinity—he regularly plunders big prizes over there—is that during his apprenticeship he spent a year working for Francois Doumen.

While Doumen can obviously train a chaser—see The Fellow and First Gold amongst others—he certainly has a knack with hurdlers too, the outstanding Baracouda instantly springing to mind, and it seems George has inherited the same touch. Module, a debut winner in a four-year-old event at Enghien on his only start for Laurent Viel, didn't enjoy much luck in races at Auteuil on his first two starts for his new yard last autumn, but was mightily impressive on his British debut. Having had a two-month break, Module showed plenty of drive and determination to wear down Art Professor in a seventeen-furlong handicap (off 130) at Cheltenham's late-January meeting, not going as well as some coming down the hill but well on top at the finish, shaping as though longer trips will show him in an even better light. Accordingly, he immediately appealed as the type who could go well in the Coral Cup at the Festival, though the scopey youngster ended up missing both Cheltenham and Aintree due to a 'minor muscle issue'. A useful looker, Module's potential for better in 2012/13 remains, whether it be

Module scoring at Cheltenham on his sole start in Britain to date

over hurdles (his new mark is 139) or fences. Module has raced on ground softer than good and promises to be suited by two and a half miles and further. ***Tom George***

Nodebateaboutit ★ h89p c117p

7 b.g Alflora (Ire) – Mystere (Ire) (Montelimar (USA))
2011/12 24s[4] 24v[6] c25s* c24s* c31s[bd] Apr 27

While it's dangerous to believe every tweet you read on Twitter, an uploaded photo to confirm his claims means we can be certain that Tom George, just one of a plethora of National Hunt racing personnel on the social networking site, took delivery in mid-August of a juvenile filly from France that has the distinction of being a half-sister to the top-class Sprinter Sacre. Undoubtedly the Gloucestershire trainer will be relishing the prospect of securing a valuable victory with Altesse Sacre in the coming seasons, but nearer to hand George will be looking to such as promising staying chaser Nodebateaboutit to provide some good days for the stable.

Having shaped better than the result suggested on all of his three starts over hurdles, Nodebateaboutit was quickly switched to fences on Boxing Day and stepped up just as his imposing physique suggested he might when landing a novice handicap at Wetherby, only ever doing enough to beat Rebel Swing. That form worked out well and it was no surprise to see Nodebateaboutit start 6/4 favourite for a four-runner similar event at Lingfield under a month later, when he again impressed in defying a 6 lb higher mark with a sound round of jumping from the front. That latest success obviously made quite an impression on Paddy Brennan, as three months later the yard's leading jockey travelled to Perth to maintain his partnership with the now tongue-tied Nodebateaboutit. Unfortunately the pair were separated three out when Nodebateaboutit was brought down, but for which he probably would have completed the hat-trick, seemingly going best at the time. Compensation for his supporters shouldn't be long in coming in the new season, when we expect Nodebateaboutit to carry on his progress over fences, and he looks a likely sort for the regional Nationals, from a staying family and clearly not short on stamina himself. He has raced only on ground softer than good so far (acts on soft). ***Tom George***

Oscara Dara (Ire) h139p

7 b.g Oscar (Ire) – Lisa's Storm (Ire) (Glacial Storm (USA))
2011/12 16s* 16d[4] 16v* Apr 27

We tend to know what we're going to get when we put forward a Nicky Henderson horse in this publication. For example, the five horses from Seven Barrows that made last season's *Fifty* won over half of their twenty starts for a combined £1 level-stakes profit just shy of £12, and they included the extremely exciting pair Sprinter Sacre and Simonsig. Similarly, Oscara Dara is expected to make a healthy contribution from the yard this season.

Oscara Dara ran with success in bumpers for Alan Fleming, but with that trainer having parted company with long-standing patron Andrew Wates in April of last year, the horse was in the care of Henderson when making his return from a year off (leg injury) in a novice hurdle at Sandown in March. Oscara Dara belied the absence in impressive fashion, trouncing a field that included favourite Cousin Khee (third) and better-fancied stablemate Zama Zama (fourth). With that impressive victory in the bag it was straight to Aintree, where Oscara Dara really gave us an indication that he was a horse to keep on the right side when a keeping-on fourth of twelve to stablemate Darlan in a Grade 2 novice (Captain Conan, also in our *Fifty*, took second). Oscara Dara, whose Irish point-winning younger brother O'Faolains Boy was sold for 100,000 guineas in April, ended his campaign when stepping up again to justify significant support in a quite valuable novice hurdle at the Punchestown Festival, running on strongly to beat another stable-companion Malt Master by three and a half lengths, with next-time-out winners in third and fourth.

That Oscara Dara achieved a useful level in little time over hurdles clearly bodes well for his chasing prospects this season, and it will be a surprise if this lengthy, angular gelding, who is closely related to useful staying chaser Saddlers Storm, doesn't prove

Useful hurdler Oscara Dara has always looked a potential chaser

at least as good over the larger obstacles. Raced only on ground softer than good so far, Oscara Dara will be suited by further than two miles. ***Nicky Henderson***

Pearls Legend h118p

5 b.g Midnight Legend – Pearl's Choice (Ire) (Deep Run)
2011/12 F16d^4 F16g^6 :: 2012/13 16g^3 20d^2 16s* Jul 11

John Spearing may be scaling down his involvement in National Hunt racing if his volume of runners in the last few years is anything to go by—twenty-eight in 2011/12, a far cry from the one hundred and one he saddled in 2008/9—but the Kinnersley trainer has a horse to look forward to this season in the form of Pearls Legend.

Having shown he was not without ability when racing prominently in a couple of Towcester bumpers in February and March, Pearls Legend made a satisfactory hurdling debut in a novice at his local track Worcester in May. Despite racing keenly and blundering three out and two out that day, Pearls Legend outran his odds of 20/1 in finishing third, looking the sort who would improve with racing. That is exactly what he did on his next two outings, both in similar events at the same course, finishing second when upped to two and a half miles next time out and then overcoming the drop back to the minimum trip to get off the mark, having four lengths in hand over subsequent winner Latest Trend.

While it can't be overlooked that Pearls Legend's jumping hasn't been the most fluent so far, we anticipate that becoming less of an issue as he gains more experience, and it's his undoubted potential combined with an opening mark of 117 that makes him a very interesting one for handicaps over timber, especially when returned to trips beyond two miles—his half-brother and dam both stayed three miles. He also possesses the size and substance to prove at least as good over fences when the time comes. ***John Spearing***

Ranjaan (Fr) ★ h140p

4 b.g Dubai Destination (USA) – Ridafa (Ire) (Darshaan)
2011/12 16s^{2} 16g^{F} 16g* 17d* Jan 19

Ranjaan's name is one which could soon be added to the long list of horses bred by the Aga Khan who have gone on to make a name for themselves over jumps in Britain and Ireland, a list which includes the Triumph Hurdle winners Shawiya, Zaynar and

Ranjaan looks open to plenty of further improvement in his second season over hurdles

Ranjaan's stablemate Zarkandar. Ranjaan himself didn't contest the Triumph, or indeed any of the championship events for juvenile hurdlers, but the form he showed when winning an all-aged handicap at Taunton on his final start last season suggests that he would have been involved in the finish had he done so.

As was the case with the aforementioned Triumph winners, Ranjaan also raced on the Flat for the Aga Khan, showing useful form at up to a mile and three quarters in France where he was trained by Mikel Delzangles. Bought for €200,000 in June 2011, Ranjaan finished a promising second on his hurdling debut five months later and went on to win both of his subsequent completed starts. After justifying favouritism in a juvenile at Kempton, Ranjaan put up a performance which was bettered by few others in his age group in 2011/12 when accounting for some useful handicappers at Taunton. Moving into contention early in the straight, Ranjaan wasn't fluent at the last two flights but extended his advantage even so, winning by three and a half lengths from Third Intention, who in turn pulled clear of the remainder. Ranjaan looks a smart prospect, one who will go on to make his mark in graded races eventually, though he could well pick up a valuable handicap before then. Indeed, he looks just the type for the race formerly known as the Greatwood at Cheltenham in November, a contest his stable won last year with the then four-year-old Brampour. ***Paul Nicholls***

Real Milan (Ire) ★ h136p

7 b.g Milan – The Real Athlete (Ire) (Presenting)
2011/12 20s* 20v* 24v^4 Feb 18

Donald McCain left it very late in reaching the one-hundred winner mark for the first time in 2010/11, but that was far from being the case in 2011/12. The century was achieved towards the end of January when Real Milan completed a four-timer for the yard at Haydock, and by season's end McCain had reached a total of one hundred and fifty three in finishing third behind Messrs Nicholls and Henderson once again, a testament to the ever-increasing strength of his stable. Given the start he's had to the latest campaign it would be no surprise to see McCain post an even quicker century and better last season's final total, weather permitting, and Real Milan looks sure to play his part once again.

Real Milan made an immediate impact over hurdles after moving to McCain from Anabel Murphy, for whom he had won at Hereford on the second of his two starts in bumpers in 2010/11. A round of jumping which could be put down to his lack of experience wasn't enough to prevent Real Milan from making a winning start in a maiden at Uttoxeter in December; and he followed up in a three-runner novice event at Haydock where he took well to the Fixed Brush hurdles in easily landing the odds. Both races were over two and a half miles, and the stoutly-bred Real Milan looked sure to be suited by the step up to three miles when returned to Haydock for the Prestige Novices' Hurdle, a Grade 2 event. As expected, Real Milan did show further improvement, finishing fourth to the subsequent Spa Novices' Hurdle winner Brindisi Breeze, though in the event his stamina was stretched, weakening after a mistake at the last. The ground was very testing and it was perhaps the case that Real Milan wasn't quite ready for such a slog at that stage of his development. Three miles or more won't be a problem another day, and he could develop into a Grand National horse in time. He certainly has the right connections for that particular race, not only trainer-wise but also where his pedigree is concerned, as his dam is from the family of Royal Athlete and West Tip. First things first, though, and it is in novice chases that the useful-looking Real Milan will be well worth following this season. ***Donald McCain***

Rocky Creek (Ire) h140

6 b.g Dr Massini (Ire) – Kissantell (Ire) (Broken Hearted)

2011/12 21g^{2} 24g* 24g Mar 16

In the entertainment world so-called supergroups rarely work out—for every Traveling Wilburys there's a dozen Blind Faith's—but in the world of business, and equine business in particular, the pooling of intelligence and wealth can often pay substantial dividends. Following the likes of smart chaser Ghizao and bumper/hurdles winner Salubrious, Rocky Creek is the latest hot prospect to represent the collaboration between two of jumps racing's most successful owners, Andy Stewart and David Johnson.

Despite failing to make his €14,000 reserve at Goffs as a three-year-old, Rocky Creek boasts a quality pedigree (his full brother Tell Massini was a useful hurdler/chaser at up to three miles) and he quickly upheld the family's good name himself when justifying 6/4 favouritism in a maiden point in Ireland in February 2011, beating his now stablemate Rolling Aces. Nine months on, and having joined current connections, Rocky Creek may have not quite lived up to his market billing (odds on) when finding Allthekingshorses a neck too good in a novice hurdle at Exeter, but in running to a useful level he stamped himself as a good prospect, one sure to win races. Stepped up to Grade 2 level in the River Don Novices' Hurdle at Doncaster three months later, Rocky Creek did just that in defeating the equally-promising Gullinbursti, powering ahead from the second last and laying down a claim to be one of the leading contenders for the Cheltenham Festival's staying novice championship event. As it turned out, Rocky Creek managed only eighth in the Spa, his inexperience seemingly an issue, but that effort is easily overlooked when considering the promise of his previous outings. Bred for the larger obstacles, the useful-looking Rocky Creek is reportedly rated one of his yard's best prospects for staying novice chases this term and has the potential to be one of the major players in that division. ***Paul Nicholls***

Rocky Creek defeating another of our Fifty, Gullinbursti, at Doncaster

Ruben Cotter (Ire) h134p

6 b.g Beneficial – Bonnie Thynes (Ire) (Good Thyne (USA))
2011/12 $21s^5$ $24v^2$ $24v^{pu}$ :: 2012/13 23d* May 8

There seems to be a growing trend of jockeys, while still employed for their expertise in the saddle, turning their hand to the purchase of bloodstock and having notable results. Perhaps the most famous is Barry Geraghty having signed the bill for his own RSA Chase hero Bobs Worth as a yearling, but Katie Walsh enjoyed pinhooking success with Gimcrack winner Caspar Netscher and Philip Enright was responsible for the €24,000 purchase of the promising Ruben Cotter as an unraced three-year-old.

Owned by Enright's father Tony and put into training with the rider's principal employer Robert Tyner, Ruben Cotter wasted little time in proving his buyer's judgement wasn't misplaced, with his two-length win in a maiden on only his second start in Irish points particularly noteworthy as the runner-up was one of last season's leading novice hurdlers Dedigout. It's probably fair to assume the Enright family then enjoyed a tidy profit from the horse's sale as he would next appear in a novice hurdle at Exeter under the care of Paul Nicholls and sporting the Viking Flagship colours of meat magnate Graham Roach. Having bettered his opening fifth when finding only Big Occasion two and three quarter lengths too good in a similar race at Chepstow just under a month later, Ruben Cotter was then cast into the deeper waters of the Grade 2 won by Brindisi Breeze at Haydock in mid-February. While a bad mistake at the eighth contributed to his disappointing effort that day, the fact that he was even in the race at all signified the regard in which he's held and it was little surprise to see him get back on an upward curve in a competitive handicap (mark of 123) back at Exeter almost three months later, when Ruben Cotter's fine-jumping defeat of the steadily progressive Water Garden showed him to be at least useful. A strong traveller who stays three miles and probably acts on heavy ground, this half-brother to the fairly useful hurdler/chasers General Kutuzov and Leading Authority is likely to continue on the up and is one to watch out for in 2012/13, when novice chases could also feature on his agenda. ***Paul Nicholls***

Salut Flo (Fr) ★ c150+

7 b.g Saint des Saints (Fr) – Royale Marie (Fr) (Garde Royale)
2011/12 c21g c21g* Mar 15

For the first time since 1999, when the Martin Pipe-trained Majadou obliged at odds of 7/4, the handicap chase at the Cheltenham Festival now known as the Byrne Group Plate went to the favourite in the latest season. Pipe's son David had nominated Salut Flo as his yard's best chance of a winner at the Festival and the well-backed 9/2-shot would have given Pipe jnr few anxious moments as he justified his trainer's faith. Salut Flo hardly saw any of his twenty-one rivals once the race was under way, sent straight to the front, jumping boldly and winning unchallenged by six lengths from The Cockney Mackem. It was a career-best effort from Salut Flo, but judged on his progress to date and the manner of his victory in such a competitive contest, there may be even better to come from this lightly-raced seven-year-old.

Successful over hurdles and fences in France before joining Pipe, Salut Flo won a handicap chase at Doncaster and finished a very good second in a similar event at Haydock in two starts for his new stable in 2009/10. Unfortunately a tendon injury kept Salut Flo off the course in 2010/11 and he was to make just the one appearance prior to the Byrne Plate. That was in December when he shaped as though retaining all of his ability in another valuable Grade 3 twenty-one furlong handicap at Cheltenham. Don't be surprised if we see Salut Flo next in a similar event at the same venue in November, namely the Paddy Power Gold Cup, a race which Martin Pipe captured on no fewer than eight occasions and which David won for the first time last season with the ill-fated Great Endeavour, also a winner of the Byrne Plate. Salut Flo, who has raced only on good ground or softer and acts on heavy, looks just the sort for the race. ***David Pipe***

Phil Turner, Handicapper (Salut Flo): *"Salut Flo really impressed me when running away with what looked a competitive handicap on paper at the Festival, and with the gelding still unexposed over fences, chances are he can land another good prize this season. The Paddy Power is the obvious starting point, and I fancy he'll be contesting graded races by the spring."*

Simonsig ★ h162p

6 gr.g Fair Mix (Ire) – Dusty Too (Terimon)
2011/12 F18g* 19g* 20s^2 18s* 21g* 20d* Apr 14

Simonsig, a member of last year's *Fifty*, exceeded even our expectations, showing himself to be an outstanding novice with four wins from five outings over timber, including a Cheltenham-Aintree double, and we expect similar big things from Nicky Henderson's gelding this time around.

A dual-winning pointer, as well as a bumper winner on his sole outing under Rules for Ian Ferguson, Simonsig's opening success over hurdles came on his debut for Henderson in a novice at Ascot in November and, after finding only the more-

We expect Simonsig to reach the very top, be it over hurdles or fences

experienced Fingal Bay too good in a Grade 2 at Sandown, he quickly got back in the winning groove in a minor event at Kelso in February, not having to match the very smart level he showed on his previous run to beat Knockara Beau easily. Simonsig had clearly impressed not only us in the embryonic stages of his hurdling career, sent off a solid 2/1 favourite in a field of seventeen for the Baring Bingham Novices' Hurdle at the Festival, and he gave his supporters few (if any) moments of worry with a flawless display, beating Felix Yonger by seven lengths and providing Henderson with a record forty-first Festival success. Exactly a month on, in the John Smith's Mersey Novices' Hurdle at Aintree, Simonsig repeated the dose, this time more than doubling his Prestbury Park margin of superiority with a defeat of Super Duty. In short, it was a near faultless first season from a horse destined for the very top.

At the time of writing, plans seem up in the air as regards which route Simonsig will take in 2012/13. A chasing type in appearance, Simonsig would clearly be a very exciting novice chase prospect, already market leader for next year's Arkle, though given that Seven Barrows have plenty of other good chasing prospects for this season as well as the more established pair of Sprinter Sacre and Finian's Rainbow, it's possible that the grey will remain over timber for one more year, in which case general quotes of 10/1 for the Champion Hurdle would soon look very generous. A strong-travelling sort, Simonsig is sure to prove as effective over two miles as he is over two and a half, perhaps even more so. ***Nicky Henderson***

Swing Bowler h120p

5 b.m Galileo (Ire) – Lady Cricket (Fr) (Cricket Ball (USA))
2011/12 F16m* F16d* 16d* 17g* Mar 18

Although the best was clearly yet to come, 2006 wasn't a bad year for young sire Galileo, as not only was he represented on the track by Group 1 winners Red Rocks, Nightime, Sixties Icon and Teofilo but the dual-Derby winner had earlier in the year covered mares that would go on to produce top-level victors Cape Blanco and Lily of The Valley. In amongst the records of that year's nominations you'll also find one Lady Cricket, a one-time top-class chaser and now the mother of Swing Bowler.

During an illustrious career that saw her only ever partnered by Tony McCoy in her twenty-two races in Britain, Lady Cricket clean bowled the opposition in the Game Spirit Chase as well as what was then the Thomas Pink Gold Cup at Cheltenham. Her time in the breeding sheds has been much less distinguished thus far, though the exploits of Swing Bowler could well help change that. On her first appearance at the crease in a Wincanton bumper in May, Swing Bowler, carrying the same green, blue and white colours of owner David Johnson that were helped made famous by the exploits of her dam, dismissed the opposition with ease before again giving her rivals the slip on her return from an autumn break in a similar event at Warwick on New Year's Eve. Switched to hurdles in a maiden at Ludlow just under two months later, Swing Bowler completed the hat-trick with the minimum of fuss, the half-length winning margin over subsequent scorer Sonoran Sands far from a fair reflection of her dominance.

Swing Bowler was perhaps fortunate to remain with perfect figures after her final outing in a novice at Newton Abbot, when benefiting from the final-hurdle departure of Sleeping City (very little in it at the time). Nevertheless, in form terms it was still a step up, as well as a clear indication that Swing Bowler is a useful mare in the making who must be kept on side in 2012/13, when defying an opening mark of 123 is likely to prove well within her capabilities. ***David Pipe***

Ted Spread h133

5 b.g Beat Hollow – Highbrook (USA) (Alphabatim (USA))
2011/12 16g^{4} 17d^{2} 17d* 16d 17g Mar 16

In Ted Spread, Paul Nicholls looked to have a horse with just the right profile to pick up the £75,000 bonus on offer for winning one of the season's most valuable handicap hurdles, the Imperial Cup at Sandown, and following up in any race at the Cheltenham

Ted Spread on his way to victory at Taunton

Festival the following week, something achieved so far only by the Pipe stable with Olympian, Blowing Wind and Gaspara. A smart performer on the Flat at up to a mile and three quarters when trained by Mark Tompkins, for whom he had also shown promise on his jumping debut in November, Ted Spread quickly developed into a useful hurdler for Nicholls. After chasing home the season's top juvenile Grumeti in a novice event at Taunton, Ted Spread, tongue tied for the first time, gave an impressive display when winning a handicap on the same course in January by seven lengths, effortlessly moving through from last to first during the hottest part of the race and merely nudged along to draw clear on the run-in.

With further improvement on the cards, Ted Spread seemed all set to strut his stuff on a much bigger stage and was sent off clear favourite for the Imperial Cup, but he not only failed to give his running in that but also in the County Hurdle six days later. Make no mistake, Ted Spread is a good deal better than he showed at either Sandown or Cheltenham, and following a breathing operation in the summer we fully expect him to resume his progress and win a good handicap in 2012/13. The rather leggy Ted Spread, who will stay beyond seventeen furlongs, put up one of his best performances on the Flat on good to firm ground and very testing conditions may not prove ideal for him over hurdles, though he coped well with good to soft at Taunton. ***Paul Nicholls***

The New One (Ire) F121

4 b.g King's Theatre (Ire) – Thuringe (FR) (Turgeon (USA))
2011/12 F14g* F14d* F16g6 F17d* Apr 14

If asked about the future exploits of any number of his horses that showed plenty of promise in bumpers, Nigel Twiston-Davies has an illustrious roll of honour from which to read. Arctic Kinsman, Beau and Mister Morose were all winners in National Hunt Flat races for the yard, as were future Hennessy winner King's Road and subsequent De Vere Gold Cup hero Frantic Tan. Add to that list the likes of Grade 2-winning hurdler Battlecry and 2010 Gold Cup winner Imperial Commander and it becomes clear that exciting prospect The New One is very much in the right hands.

It's safe to assume that The New One has always been highly regarded at home, sent off 11/4 favourite in a field of sixteen when making his debut in a three-year-old event at Warwick in November, and he had little trouble seeing off Dalavar by two and three quarter lengths. Just under two months later The New One defied a penalty in a listed contest at Cheltenham, beating promising Haydock winner Chancery. The angular gelding, who had been purchased for €25,000 in Ireland five months prior to his first racecourse appearance, would then go on to improve further on each of his two subsequent starts, bettering his staying-on sixth to Champagne Fever in the Champion Bumper at Cheltenham when outbattling My Tent Or Yours to land the equivalent event at Aintree a month later. The way The New One has travelled and battled in his races so far, particularly when recording his latest victory, certainly bodes well and, having reached a smart level in bumpers, we'll be disappointed if The New One isn't extremely competitive in some of the better novice hurdles over two miles plus in 2012/13. ***Nigel Twiston-Davies***

Twelve Roses F106

4 ch.g Midnight Legend – Miniature Rose (Anshan)
2011/12 F16d* Apr 14

After a few lean years, the Kim Bailey yard look to be back on the up if their tally for the last two seasons is anything to go by. Bailey's runners recorded level stakes profits in both 2010/11 (38 winners at a 19% strike rate) and 2011/12 (32 winners at 15%), and we expect Twelve Roses to contribute to another successful campaign for the stable this time round.

Twelve Roses has a pedigree which screams stamina, being a brother to the same connections' fairly useful hurdler Cinderella Rose (stays two and three quarter miles) out of a half-sister to the useful staying hurdler/winning chaser Ringaroses, and that he was able to make a winning debut in a bumper has to be deemed very encouraging. Despite having unshipped the yard's 7-lb claimer Ed Cookson at the start at Chepstow, 15/2-shot Twelve Roses impressed greatly in the race itself, travelling fluently and getting into things easily, before knuckling down well to get on top of the Philip Hobbs-trained runner-up Turanjo Bello despite edging left through inexperience. The fact the third had little problem landing a similar race next time highlights that it was probably a fair race for the grade and one which we expect to produce more winners.

Bailey is at the forefront of trainer's using the internet and social networking to promote their yards, and we know from reading his daily blogs and newsletters that the plans for Twelve Roses following his victory were to be 'schooled in the art of jumping before heading out to grass for a good summer holiday.' The trainer added that 'he is a horse with a very bright future'. We certainly believe so too and we feel he'll have no trouble defying a penalty before his attentions are turned to hurdling, with two and a half miles and further likely to suit in that sphere. ***Kim Bailey***

Ulis de Vassy (Fr) h115p

4 b.g Voix du Nord (Fr) – Helathou (Fr) (Video Rock (Fr))
2011/12 16m 17v^{pu} 17v* Dec 19

It was straight to hurdling for Ulis de Vassy, even though his pedigree might have suggested that he had a future on the Flat or that he would at least be started off in bumpers. By the smart French middle-distance performer and dual-Group 1 winner

Voix du Nord, Ulis de Vassy is the fourth foal of a mare who was successful three times around a mile and a half in France and who has produced a winner over a similar distance there.

A juvenile hurdle at Uttoxeter in October is where Ulis de Vassy made his debut and his inexperience showed there, particularly in his jumping, so it was hardly a surprise that he could make no impact in a much hotter race at Auteuil just a month later. It was a very different story when Ulis de Vassy made his third appearance, though. With his stable in much better form than it was earlier in the season, Ulis de Vassy was sent off second favourite for a seven-runner juvenile event at Bangor in December and justified the support in a race run in very testing conditions. Jumping more fluently than previously, Ulis de Vassy travelled strongly up with the pace before asserting two out and, though idling on the run-in, had a length and a half to spare over Mentalist at the line, the pair clear of the fairly useful Colebrooke. Back in fourth was hurdling debutant Kian's Delight who has gone on to show himself useful, winning the Summer Champion Hurdle (Handicap) at Perth in August. That form points to a mark of 112 underestimating Ulis de Vassy's ability and it is one he can exploit to the full when he makes his handicap debut, while it could be difficult for the official assessor to catch up with him as he looks sure to go on improving for some time to come. ***Nick Williams***

War Poet ★ h110+

5 b.g Singspiel (Ire) – Summer Sonnet (Baillamont (USA))
2011/12 16d⁴ 16m² 16s⁴ Dec 27

Ex-jumps jockey David O'Meara featured as a 'Future Star' in this publication last year and, whilst not wanting to appear too self-congratulatory, it's fair to say the County Cork native now based in North Yorkshire hasn't let us down in the ensuing period. Viva Colonia, who was a 14/1 winner of a listed handicap at Market Rasen, was one of his stars over hurdles last season and we're confident War Poet can follow suit this term.

Despite being bred in the purple—he's a half-brother to Group 1 winner Act One amongst a host of other black-type performers—the Darley-bred War Poet was picked up for just £2,200 as a three-year-old. However, he proved a success in his debut season when winning a brace of mile and a half handicaps on the Flat, showing himself to be useful. While War Poet's first taste of hurdling hardly suggested he was a winner waiting to happen (well-held fourth of five in a listed novice at Haydock), he obviously benefited significantly from that experience, finishing a close second to Gogeo in a novice at Doncaster just a week later. War Poet again shaped better than the result when fourth of thirteen to Embsay Crag in a similar race at Wetherby on his final start, simply suffering for a lack of stamina in testing conditions having been going as well as any of his rivals up until the final flight. War Poet has since added to his tally during the latest Flat season, winning a mile and a quarter handicap at Doncaster, and he strikes as the type to make hay in handicaps around the minimum trip when returning to hurdles, bearing in mind both his Flat form and the promise he's shown over timber so far. He has won on the Flat on soft ground, though it's possible less testing conditions may see him to best effect over hurdles. ***David O'Meara***

Wings of Icarus (Ire) h105p

5 ch.g Cut Quartz (Fr) – Moody Cloud (Fr) (Cyborg (Fr))
2011/12 F18d* 20s^6 20s^4 16s^3 Mar 8

The story of Icarus and his wings of feathers and wax is a staple of Greek Mythology, offering a prophetic insight into failed ambition above all else. While it's probably far-fetched to believe that Wings of Icarus will ever fly as high as his high-class half-brothers Quito de La Roque and Kazal, we certainly expect him to reach greater heights this season than he did last.

Having dead-heated in a maiden point in Ireland in May 2011, Wings of Icarus made a successful debut for David Pipe and owner's Shirl and The Girls (David Johnson's wife Shirley, his daughter Lisa and daughter-in-law Claire) in a bumper at Plumpton in November, justifying favouritism with a neck defeat of Cinevator (won handicap hurdle off 107 subsequently). Wings of Icarus' attentions were quickly switched to hurdling, and while it can't be said that he has stood out in three starts in maidens—easily his best effort came when nine and a quarter lengths fourth of eleven to Holywell at Chepstow—he looked distinctly green for the most part and definitely offered something to work with, his final effort easily forgiven as he was turned out quickly and presented with an inadequate test of stamina. On the whole, Wings of Icarus, whose pedigree suggests he may well be better over further than two and a half miles, remains with potential heading into handicap hurdles, where there's a good chance that an opening mark of 107 will underestimate him. ***David Pipe***

Martin Dixon, Chief Reporter (Wings Of Icarus): *"Simply put, this horse could well be thrown-in off an official mark of 107, and I wouldn't be surprised to see him rack up a sequence this term. Last season was all about laying a platform, but he still showed plenty of promise, and his pedigree is a strong pointer for much better to come. The yard have an excellent record with similar types over the years, too."*

SECTION 2

Aupcharlie (Ire) h133p

6 b.g Daliapour (Ire) – Lirfa (USA) (Lear Fan (USA))
2011/12 F16g 16v³ 16d² 20d* Jan 28

In case it should ever come up in a racing quiz, when Dr Machini won a Fairyhouse bumper in mid-January she became the first winner trained by Willie Mullins to carry the emerald green, yellow and red silks of increasingly prominent owners Alan and Ann Potts. While that mare is certainly open to further improvement over timber, the partnership looks set to enjoy plenty more success with another unexposed hurdler in Aupcharlie.

Given his pedigree (by a Coronation Cup winner, from the family of Prix de Diane heroine Latice), it was no surprise Aupcharlie did very well in bumpers for trainer Patrick Collins, building on his win at Naas when finishing a useful third to Cheltenian in the Cheltenham Champion Bumper of 2010/11. However, he's also a brother to the smart French hurdler La Grande Dame, and in three runs in maiden hurdles since joining his current yard Aupcharlie has shown himself to be at least useful. Placed at Thurles (best effort when third to Lord Windermere) in November and Leopardstown (tongue tied, second to The Way We Were) in December, Aupcharlie got off the mark in a twelve-runner event at the latter track the following month, travelling and jumping well close up before staying on to defeat Whispering Hills. While he'll surely pay his way over fences in time, Aupcharlie looks well treated for handicap hurdles off an opening mark of 127, and he also appeals as the type to relish a step up to three miles. Aupcharlie has done all his racing on ground good or softer, with his best performance coming on heavy. ***Willie Mullins***

Ballynacree (Ire) h131p

4 b.g Westerner – Noeleen's Choice (Ire) (Montelimar (USA)
2011/12 16v* 16d² 16d* Apr 10)

To say connections were caught unawares when Ballynacree made a successful debut in a seventeen-runner juvenile maiden hurdle at Gowran in February is probably an understatement. The mount of 7-lb claimer Jody McGarvey, who had ridden his first winner just over two weeks earlier, the gelding went off at 40/1 and was almost three times that price on the Tote. The manner of Ballynacree's victory made it all the more surprising that he came in for no support in the market, looking a good prospect as he cruised into contention before quickening six lengths clear on the run-in. Two subsequent efforts confirmed that Ballynacree was a well-above average juvenile. Ballynacree gave best only to another promising type, Lord Windermere, in a novice event at Naas; and he then won the Grade 3

Ballynacree appeals as the type to do even better over fences

Weatherbys Ireland GSB Hurdle when returned to his own age group at Fairyhouse. With Tony McCoy on board for the first time, Ballynacree showed a good attitude in winning by a length and a quarter from Gorgeous Sixty at Fairyhouse, leading under hands and heels between the last two and responding well to see off the challenge of the runner-up.

Ballynacree will certainly go on and win more races if kept to hurdling, but it's as a chaser that he is going to make a name for himself. His dam is a half-sister to Risk Accessor who did most of his racing for Ballynacree's owner and trainer J. P. McManus and Christy Roche, developing into a smart chaser at up to three miles. Ballynacree, who is bred to be suited by two and a half miles and more, has the potential to reach an even higher standard. ***Christy Roche***

Buckers Bridge (Ire) F124

6 b.g Pelder (Ire) – La Fiere Dame (Ire) (Lafontaine (USA))
2011/12 F18s* F16v* Apr 26

Honesty has certainly proved to be the best policy for Henry de Bromhead. So the story goes, towards the end of 2004 the trainer received a call from Alan Potts inquiring into the possible purchase of the trainer's promising young pointer

The sky's the limit for Buckers Bridge following two impressive wins in bumpers

Oscar India, but before a deal could be agreed the horse injured a tendon. The founder of the Derbyshire-based mining and quarrying company MMD Group was consequently informed that he couldn't possibly be sold the horse and that maybe he would like to choose from two others. While further bad fortune ultimately prevented Potts' two new acquisitions from reaching their potential a partnership was established nevertheless, one that would go on to have notable success with Sizing Europe amongst others.

Champion Chase hero Sizing Europe only ran to a fair level in three starts in bumpers, whereas Potts' latest recruit, Buckers Bridge, showed himself to be very smart in that sphere during his first season under Rules. Having already justified 6/4 favouritism in a maiden on his sole start in points, it was perhaps no surprise to see Buckers Bridge sent off the 4/1 second choice of the market when making his debut in a point-to-point bumper at Gowran in December. Staying on strongly having been ridden over a furlong out, Buckers Bridge ultimately scored with plenty in hand over runner-up More Madness (winner of a similar race subsequently), with the rest a further seventeen lengths adrift. While that victory suggested he had all the hallmarks of a nice stayer in the making, Buckers Bridge really got the pulse racing on his only start after. Again partnered by amateur Davy Roche, he drew right away from a clutch of useful performers, headed by Morning Royalty, in a twelve-runner bumper at the Punchestown Festival in late-April. While Buckers

Bridge clearly has the potential to head right to the top of the novice hurdling tree this season, in the aftermath of Punchestown connections appeared to be contemplating the idea of sending their exciting prospect straight over fences, and there's no doubt he has the physique to suggest he'll prove very effective at that game, too. He's an exciting prospect. ***Henry de Bromhead***

Clashnabrook (Ire) h114 c74p

7 b.g Alderbrook – Cappard Ridge (Ire) (Executive Perk)
2011/12 c16v^5 c17s 16s 21v* 21s^3 20v* 20v* 20v Apr 23

While Royal Mail honoured Great Britain's gold medallists at this summer's London Olympic Games by painting one of its iconic red post boxes gold in each athlete's home town, connections of Clashnabrook, named after an area near trainer Eoghan O'Grady's Ballycushen base, may soon do something similar to celebrate their local hero with more success predicted for the stable star this season.

After showing very little to enthuse over in his first six racecourse appearances, Clashnabrook landed an old-fashioned gamble (returned 8/1 having been available at 25/1 in the morning) in a handicap hurdle (mark of 81) at Limerick in December, and then proceeded to win two of his next three outings in similar races, both at Fairyhouse. On the latter occasion, Clashnabrook showed form bordering on fairly useful in beating King of The Refs in a novice event, despite idling on the run-in. However, while Clashnabrook can probably still achieve more over hurdles—his final effort forgiven coming at the end of a long season—it's his scope for better over fences that makes him so appealing. Clashnabrook ran to only a poor level in two outings over the larger obstacles at the beginning of last season but it's difficult to believe that was the limit of his ability, the theory backed up by both his physique (big and workmanlike) and pedigree (from the family of top-class hurdler turned very smart chaser Time For Rupert). With that in mind, we expect connections to exploit Clashnabrook's chase mark of 82 (rated 29 lb higher over hurdles) in 2012/13, with the strong-travelling hold-up performer especially suited by races in which they go a good pace. ***Eoghan O'Grady***

Dedigout (Ire) h150p

6 b.g Bob Back (USA) – Dainty Daisy (Ire) (Buckskin (Fr))
2011/12 F17g^2 20s* 20v* 20v^3 22d* 20v* Apr 27

There's no doubt that the County Meath yard of Tony Martin has received an injection of quality in recent years, with last year's figures in terms of wins and total prize money not far off the highs of 2007/08. The exploits of top-level scorers

Dedigout (left) looks a fine chasing prospect following an impressive debut season over timber

Dedigout and Bog Warrior, comfortably Martin's two highest earners in 2011/12, have helped raise the yard to the next level and no doubt cemented a partnership with Michael O'Leary's Gigginstown House Stud that will continue to bear fruit for many seasons to come.

Dedigout, who had changed hands for just €5,000 as a three-year-old having fetched over three times that as a foal, actually finished runner-up to Paul Nicholls' useful hurdler Ruben Cotter on his only start in points before joining Martin. The half-brother to three-mile hurdle winner Winning Counsel would then confirm his abundant promise when filling the same position in a Punchestown bumper on his debut for current connections. Quickly switched to hurdles, Dedigout's form soon bordered on smart, winning a maiden at the same track in November and a novice at Navan the following month, looking a stayer of tremendous potential. Dedigout managed only third to Monksland in a Grade 2 at Naas on his next outing, when let down by his jumping, but in two subsequent starts (with a tongue tie fitted) he showed in no uncertain terms that he was one of the best Irish-trained novices. A success in what looked a strong open handicap at Fairyhouse was first up, and Dedigout then took the return to graded company in his stride by landing the Grade 1 Champion Novice Hurdle at Punchestown, raising his Timeform rating again when staying on strongly to beat Colour Squadron by two lengths.

The highly exciting Dedigout certainly has the physique (big, deep-girthed) to prove at least as effective if not better over fences and, having proved he relishes heavy ground, there has to be a strong possibility he could follow in the hoofprints of Bog Warrior in winning the Drinmore Chase at Fairyhouse in early-December. Ultimately, however, he will be suited by three miles. ***Tony Martin***

Don Cossack (Ger) F128

5 br.g Sholokhov (Ire) – Depeche Toi (Ger) (Konigsstuhl (Ger)
2011/12 F16g[5] F19v* F16s* F16d* Apr 9

He might not have appeared in any of the acknowledged championship events, but by our reckoning Don Cossack was the best horse to compete in bumpers in 2011/12 and he promises to make a big name for himself over jumps in the seasons to come. Bought privately by Michael O'Leary after his debut and transferred from Eddie Hales to Gordon Elliott, Don Cossack was unbeaten in three subsequent starts, the first of those run over nineteen furlongs on heavy ground at Naas. Barely off the bridle in winning by eighteen lengths there, Don Cossack continued his progress back at two miles, following up in a Grade 2 event at Navan where he came from a seemingly-impossible position to peg back long-time leader Rory O'Moore.

The performance which established Don Cossack as the season's leading bumper performer came at Fairyhouse in April. Set to concede weight to all eleven of his rivals, five of them previous winners, Don Cossack made light of his task, travelling strongly as he led the chasing pack, soon in control once he made his move in the straight and pulling seventeen lengths clear. Don Cossack looked better the further he went, and although he is a half-brother to the winning two-mile hurdler Dubai King (by Dashing Blade) and features prominently in the ante-post betting for the 2013 Supreme Novices', it could be that the Baring Bingham, run over twenty-one furlongs, will be a more suitable race for him at the Cheltenham Festival. ***Gordon Elliott***

Flemenstar (Ire) c163+

7 b.g Flemensfirth (USA) – Different Dee (Ire) (Beau Sher)
2011/12 20g[4] c16s[2] c17s* c16v* c17s* c20d* c20g* Apr 8

The Cheltenham Gold Cup is the main objective for the best two Irish novice chasers of 2011/12, Sir des Champs and Flemenstar, but the ante-post betting on the event doesn't reflect that there was very little to choose between the pair in terms of form in their first season over fences, with Flemenstar's odds generally around double those of Sir des Champs, who heads the market. That Sir des Champs has been successful on both of his appearances at the Cheltenham Festival might go some way to explaining the discrepancy. Flemenstar, on the

Flemenstar will win more good races in his second season over fences

other hand, has yet to race outside of Ireland. Apparently he held no Cheltenham entries last season because he had been considered a poor traveller, though his trainer now appears to have no worries about Flemenstar on that score.

The lightly-raced Flemenstar made great strides following a promising second to Bog Warrior at Navan on his debut over fences and was unbeaten in five starts, his last three wins coming in graded events. The first of those was the Arkle Novice at Leopardstown in January, a race which Flemenstar turned into a procession, winning by nineteen lengths from Gift of Dgab. The much anticipated rematch with Bog Warrior in a three-runner Grade 3 novice at Naas proved an anti-climax, as the latter was patently amiss. Still, Flemenstar could do no more than win easily, and he went on to round off his campaign with a tremendously impressive performance in the Powers Gold Cup at Fairyhouse, jumping impeccably in winning by eleven lengths from Rathlin. On ground less testing than he had encountered previously over fences, Flemenstar travelled as though he wouldn't be at all inconvenienced by a return to shorter than two and a half miles. His pedigree, on the other hand—from the family of Welsh National winner Carvill's Hill and Becher Chase hero Samlee—reads very much like that of a staying chaser, one who should stay at least three miles. There will certainly be no shortage of options for Flemenstar in the coming months, and he looks sure to win more good races in Ireland before he tackles the Gold Cup. ***Peter Casey***

Glens Melody (Ire) F110p

4 b.f King's Theatre (Ire) – Glens Music (Ire) (Orchestra)
2011/12 F17v* :: 2012/13 F18g* F16s* Jun 7

Retirement still looks some way off for the admirable Quevega, who all being well will be going for her fifth successive win in the David Nicholson Hurdle at Cheltenham next March, but when it does come Willie Mullins might have a mare in his stable capable of filling her shoes. While Glens Melody has a long way to go before she can be considered anywhere near good enough for such a role, she does looks an exciting hurdling prospect having impressed in winning all three of her starts in bumpers.

Glens Melody made her debut in a twenty-three runner event for fillies and mares at Punchestown at the end of April and put up a taking performance in winning it from her shorter-priced stablemate Tasitiocht, who was also successful on her next two starts. Patiently ridden, Glens Melody weaved her way through to lead inside the final furlong and was three and a half lengths clear and still going away at the line. The form proved strong and Glens Melody didn't need to step up on it to land the odds at Sligo in May and Tipperary the following month, unextended when beating St Maxime seven and a half lengths on the latter course. Glens Melody, who will stay at least two and a half miles, has the physique to make a jumper and is also bred for the job: a daughter of the useful hurdler and fairly useful chaser Glens Music, she is a half-sister to the useful hurdler Ceol Rua and to the useful hurdler and fairly useful chaser Quietly Fancied. ***Willie Mullins***

Knockfierna (Ire) c146p

7 b.m Flemensfirth (USA) – Garden Town (Ire) (Un Desperado (Fr))
2011/12 20g* 24g c20s^{6} c20s2 c19s* c17s* c20v^{ro} c20v* c22v* Mar 18

Ireland has produced a number of high-profile female chasers down the years including the iconic Dawn Run, the Ferdy Murphy-ridden Arkle heroine Analogs Daughter and, more recently, Irish National winner Bluesea Cracker and Galway Plate victor Blazing Tempo. The cream of the current crop is undoubtedly Charles Byrnes' Knockfierna, who we expect to dominate her own sex again this season.

Knockfierna may take her name from a County Limerick village famous for a public appearance by a pair of leprechauns in the autumn of 1938 but her useful performances on the track are far from mythical, the pot of gold at the end of the then hurdler's rainbow in 2010/11 a defeat of Golden Sunbird in a Grade 2 at Fairyhouse. Switched to fences in late-October, Knockfierna took three starts before she got her head in front, but didn't need to match her hurdles form to land the odds in a maiden at Wexford. However, it was Knockfierna's exploits thereafter that really showed she has the class to stamp her authority on the top female-only events this term, with the prospect of picking up a Grade 1 in open company by no means beyond the realms of possibility. With wins in Grade 3 mares novices at Cork in December (beat Shop Dj), Thurles in January (beat Belle Brook) and Limerick in March (again jumped soundly when proving too good for Special Token), Knockfierna's winning streak was broken only by an unfortunate incident where she ran out approaching the second last having looked like giving the unbeaten Sir des Champs a fright in a Grade 2 at Limerick in December. With dual heavy-ground winner Knockfierna, who stays two and three quarter miles but is effective at shorter, having shown no signs of temperament either prior to or after that mishap, we have no hesitation recommending her as one to stick with in 2012/13. ***Charles Byrnes***

Micks (Ire) h109+ c–p

6 b.g Dr Massini (Ire) – Ear To The Ground (Ire) (Roselier (Fr))

2011/12 24g 16g[6] 16s 16s 20g 20v[2] 24s* 22v c16d :: 2012/13 c22g c17g May 15

Although the recent run of duck eggs suggests otherwise, Micks is a very straightforward selection to explain being a Christy Roche-trained, J. P. McManus-owned fair winning hurdler who has the potential to do a lot better in handicaps over fences from what is likely to be a lenient opening mark.

A winner of a maiden for John Halley on the second of two starts in points, Micks made his debut under Rules for current connections in a maiden hurdle at Punchestown in May 2011. The son of a winning hurdler/chaser then showed himself to be fair in his seven subsequent outings over timber, more or less progressing with each run until his final one (reportedly finished lame), clearly well suited by the step up to three miles when landing a big-field handicap at Gowran in late-November from the now useful Novarov. Micks three outings in maidens over fences haven't been totally without promise for all he was ultimately well beaten, and it will be a big disappointment should he not land at least one handicap, with his Curragh-based yard always worth looking out for in such events. Micks, whose sire's leading performers Master Medic, Fix The Rib and Massini's Maguire were all better over fences than hurdles, will be suited by the return to two and a half miles plus and he acts on heavy ground. ***Christy Roche***

Our Vinnie (Ire) h95p F106

5 b.g Vinnie Roe (Ire) – Boopsey (Ire) (Old Vic)

2011/12 F16s^{3} F16s^{3} F20d^{2} F19s* :: 2012/13 16v Sep 19

Statistics show that County Limerick trainer Charles Byrnes does particularly well with hurdlers, his numbers of winners in that sphere in Ireland over the last five seasons very nearly three times his overall amount of chase scorers in the same period. Following on from the likes of Solwhit, Pittoni and Trifolium as a good hurdling prospect for the yard is useful bumper performer Our Vinnie, who shaped with plenty of promise on his debut over timber in mid-September.

Although it took Our Vinnie four starts to get off the mark in bumpers, his victory, in a maiden event at Naas in January, was much deserved. That he had only a nose to spare over The Crafty Butcher at the line wasn't really a true reflection of his superiority either, likely to have won more easily if asked to press on earlier. Strictly on the figures, Our Vinnie's best performance actually came on his previous outing when relishing the increased test of stamina to finish a length-and-a-half second to Ballycase at Leopardstown, a race in which he had a couple of next-time-out winners well behind. Those two efforts in particular marked Our Vinnie down as one to keep on side, and the promise of his hurdling debut in a maiden at Listowel did little to alter that impression, for all he managed only seventh coming back off an eight-month break (easy to back), jumping adequately and keeping on without being given at all a hard time, the drop back to two miles probably against him. Our Vinnie is open to significant improvement over timber, especially when tackling trips of two and a half miles or more, and it will be a surprise if he doesn't better his bumper form in due course. ***Charles Byrnes***

Pageboy (Ire) h135p

4 ch.g Galileo (Ire) – Last Love (Ire) (Danehill (USA))

2011/12 16s6 16s* :: 2012/13 16d* Aug 26

Although now known as an Irish Classic-winning Flat trainer who enjoys a close association with the Coolmore partners (he married John Magnier's daughter Kate in 2002), David Wachman actually set out with the jumps firmly in mind in 1996 and went on to enjoy success with the likes of Grade 2-winning novice chaser Cane Brake. Wachman's runners over jumps are much rarer these days, but in just three starts over hurdles the same connections' Pageboy has already shown useful form, and he looks just the type to go higher still over timber in his second season.

Pageboy showed just fair form in three starts on the Flat at two and three years up to a mile and a half but once switched to hurdles looked a different proposition.

Having made an encouraging hurdling debut in a maiden at Gowran in March, Pageboy improved sufficiently five weeks later to defeat next-time-out winner E Mac in a similar event at Tipperary, quickening before the last and able to be eased close home. That strong-travelling performance suggested there was plenty more to come from Pageboy and he duly stepped up a good bit when next seen four months later, showing useful form in readily justifying 11/10 favouritism in a minor event at Cork, quickening clear to beat White Feathers by eight and a half lengths. Pageboy may be a half-brother to a US six-furlong winner, out of a dam who was fairly useful over seven, but he has obviously inherited plenty of stamina from his outstanding sire, whose progeny to have raced over jumps are headed by the notable hurdlers Celestial Halo, Galileo's Choice and Via Galilei. On a steep upward curve, Pageboy showed near-useful form when runner-up in a maiden on the Flat in late-September, and he looks just the type to land a good prize over hurdles in the coming months. ***David Wachman***

Robbie McMahon (Ire) h91+

7 b.g City Honours (USA) – Spancilhill Melody (Ire) (Lord Americo)
2011/12 16v 16v 20g Mar 4

With recent stable stars Becauseicouldntsee and Gonebeyondrecall part of a long list of Noel Glynn-trained horses to take their names from song lyrics you probably won't be surprised to learn that Robbie McMahon was a local Irish folk singer and composer in the late 1930s and '40s, who is most famous for his association with the haunting ballad 'Spancil Hill'.

We have to confess that Robbie McMahon's form figures under Rules—beaten no less than twenty-one lengths on each of his three starts in maiden hurdles—hardly inspire confidence. However, he's still very much on our radar when considering both his point form and the fact that his trainer is currently showing a level-stakes profit of £27 (to a £1 stake) in Irish handicap hurdles over the last five seasons. Out of a point-winning dam, Robbie McMahon won the last two of his three outings in that sphere himself, the way he jumped on the latter occasion pointing to him having a bright future ahead. Still in the early days of his career, we're confident Robbie McMahon will prove a different proposition once switched to handicap hurdles, where his opening mark of 95 is likely to underestimate him. He stays two and a half miles. ***Noel Glynn***

Simenon (Ire) h145+

5 b.g Marju (Ire) – Epistoliere (Ire) (Alzao (USA))
2011/12 18s[5] 16v* 16v[2] 16g 16s[3] :: 2012/13 16g* May 25

While the likes of Frankel and Black Caviar were quickening the pulses of Flat racing fans in Berkshire across five days in June, the exploits of Simenon at Royal Ascot were providing further evidence of the skill and versatility of Ireland's leading jumps trainer, Willie Mullins.

Purchased for 60,000 guineas at Tattersalls as a yearling, Simenon began his career with Andrew Balding and showed himself to be useful on the Flat in a fifteen-race spell with the Classic-winning trainer. With that level of ability allied to the fact that he numbers useful chaser Aigle d'Or amongst his family members, it was little surprise to see Simenon translate his form to timber pretty instantly for Willie Mullins having made an encouraging debut early last December. A month on from that Simenon improved massively to hammer Party Rock in a heavy-ground maiden at Cork, and even better was to follow, finding only Trifolium too good in a Grade 2 at Punchestown in February and then finishing third behind County Hurdle hero Alderwood and Trifolium in a Grade 1 at the same track's Festival in April. Four weeks later Simenon elevated his form to a smart level with a second wide-margin success over two miles at Cork, this time proving fifteen lengths better than Dazzling Susie in a minor event, cruising clear. Simenon's performances over jumps alone suggest he's a horse going places, though his efforts on the Flat over the summer have added a new dimension to his profile, achieving the notable Ascot Stakes - Queen Alexandra Stakes double at the Royal meeting and running with credit in a number of top staying contests thereafter, including a fifth in the Irish St Leger. His profile now looks very similar to that of Ile de Re, one of our *Fifty*, as both appear potentially well treated heading into handicap hurdles, in Simenon's case off a mark of 147. The strong-travelling Simenon, who has tackled only good ground or softer over hurdles (acts on heavy) but has form on good to firm on the level, will certainly stay two and a half miles over timber, with his Royal Ascot victories achieved over the same trip and beyond. ***Willie Mullins***

Woodville Lady (Ire) h118p

6 b.m Oscar (Ire) – Woodville Princess (Ire) (Torus)
2011/12 16s[3] 16v* Jan 1

Since taking out a licence to train in 1996, former champion Irish Flat jockey Christy Roche has struck up a notable partnership with J. P. McManus, with the Epsom and Irish Derby-winning rider enjoying his first Cheltenham Festival victory with the McManus-owned Khayrawani in the 1999 Coral Cup. The pair have also combined with high-class hurdler/smart chaser Youlneverwalklone and smart hurdler/Grade 1-winning chaser Like-A-Butterfly in the period since, and will be looking to Woodville Lady to provide further success in the season ahead.

A sister to winning hurdler/fairly useful chaser Wheels Up (barely stays twenty-one furlongs) and bred on the same direct cross as the useful chaser Fabalu and fairly useful hurdlers Druids Castle and Off The Ground, Woodville Lady made a highly encouraging debut when third, beaten just over five lengths, to the useful bumper performer Reizovic in a maiden hurdle at Naas in mid-November, finishing well after making an eye-catching move from mid-field early in the straight. Just nineteen days later Woodville Lady built on that promise when proving too good for subsequent winner Double Double in a similar heavy-ground contest at Fairyhouse, full of running when switched to the outer before the last and able to overcome a slightly awkward landing to win in the style of a useful prospect. Thoroughly unexposed, Woodville Lady is sure to be winning more races over hurdles, with races against her own sex likely to prove an especially fruitful hunting ground. ***Christy Roche***

SECTION 3

THE BIG-NAME INTERVIEW

Donald McCain

Donald McCain

It can often be difficult when an offspring attempts to follow in the footsteps of an illustrious parent, but since taking over the reins at Cholmondeley from his late father Ginger in 2006, Donald McCain has taken his Cheshire yard to another level, to the extent where it is now the dominant jumping force in the North of England. With a seasonal tally of winners that has increased every year for the past six, McCain has propelled himself into the upper echelons of the National Hunt training ranks, finishing 2011/12 a clear third in the trainers' championship, with only Messrs Nicholls and Henderson above him. It is not just the quantity of winners that have been boosted in recent times, the quality of the stable's horses has also been on a sharp upward curve, with current inhabitants including Grand National winner Ballabriggs, Cheltenham Festival scorers Cinders And Ashes and Peddlers Cross, and smart dual-purpose horses such as Ile de Re and Overturn. Add into the mix a strong influx of new talent for the upcoming season, particularly a large batch of ex-Irish point winners, and it would be a surprise if those statistics aren't improved yet further. The riding talent at McCain's disposal, led by the ever-dependable Jason Maguire, is more than a match for the equine variety, and with hopes high that last seasons' total of 153 winners is within reach, McCain was kind enough to provide us with an insight into some of his main players for the months ahead.

Cinders And Ashes on his way to landing the Supreme Novices' Hurdle at Cheltenham

Hurdlers

Cinders And Ashes (h152p) 5 b.g Beat Hollow – Moon Search (Rainbow Quest (USA)) 2011/12 16g² 17v* 16v* 16v* 16g* Mar 13 With Overturn going chasing he should hopefully be our Champion Hurdle horse for the season. I don't think he got the credit he deserved for winning the Supreme, I think people need to go back and watch the race to see how easily he won, he's fairly bolted in. We didn't want to hit the front too soon with him, so it was always the plan if we could take it up at the last or just after the last, but Jason got there a few strides too soon and he's made a mistake, but he's still won, and the first thing Jason said to me walking back is 'this lad hasn't had a race'. He has so much speed and he's very good over his hurdles, the two mistakes he made at Cheltenham were because he was going too well. We will probably start off at Newcastle in the Fighting Fifth. It has worked before, we have won the last two renewals with Peddlers Cross and Overturn so there is no reason not to start there.

Peddlers Cross (Ire) (c147) 7 b.g Oscar (Ire) – Patscilla (Squill (USA)) 2011/12 c17d* c17s* c16g² c20g Mar 15 Things didn't go to plan over fences last season after a promising beginning, so we are looking at starting him back over hurdles, which will more than likely be at Ascot in the two-and-a-half mile race we took last year with Overturn (Coral Hurdle). Hopefully that run will tell us whether he steps up or comes back in trip, although I think we are likely to explore longer distances subject to Ascot going well. He's settling better as he gets older which will help. I am sure all the ability is still there, we've seen him do things at home that will scare you to death.

Ile de Re (Fr) (h121+) 6 gr.g Linamix (Fr) – Ile Mamou (Ire) (Ela-Mana-Mou) 2011/12 17v^3 19d^2 16s* 16d* 16d Mar 10 Did us proud on the Flat this summer, winning both the Chester Cup and the Northumberland Plate, where he had to be very tough after being forced to race five wide. I thought he won there despite everything. He's had break since, and the owner wants him to have one more run on the Flat, so he is going to go for the Long Distance Cup on Champions Day at Ascot. There is no doubt he is well handicapped over hurdles, so maybe the race formerly known as the Greatwood would be a good starting point. I don't think there is any point wasting his handicap mark on an average race. Even if he doesn't prove as good over hurdles, it is worth finding out in that class of race. He is sure to want further than two miles, but in those top-quality handicaps over that distance, it is a bonus if you have got a low weight and you stay well.

Son of Flicka (h143) 8 b.g Groom Dancer (USA) – Calendula (Be My Guest (USA)) 2011/12 24g 16g 20v 21g 21g* 24d^F Apr 12 The Cheltenham Festival, where he was runner-up in 2011 before winning last year in the Coral Cup, is once again top of his agenda. What happens before that I'm not sure, but all roads lead back to Cheltenham. He's been a wonderful little horse for us who always does his best. It was nice to get one proper day at him last season and it was great when it came off. It's a real challenge

Son of Flicka on his way to landing a gamble in the Coral Cup at Cheltenham

and something my dad taught me, targeting one horse at one particular day. I'm not a massive fan of putting all my eggs in one basket because if it doesn't work then it's your whole season gone, but if you do it right and you succeed, then obviously it's hugely satisfying. He really came to himself in the last couple of weeks before Cheltenham and appears something of a spring horse. I think when the time comes he will be entered in the Martin Pipe, the Coral Cup and the Pertemps. The three miles of the Pertemps might suit as he was just in top gear all the way this year. He's such a tough horse, you only have to look at the way he carries his head to see that.

Lexi's Boy (Ire) (h138) 4 gr.g Verglas (Ire) – Jazan (Ire) (Danehill (USA)) 2011/12 $16d^{pu}$ 16s* 16v3 $17v^{2}$ 16g* 16g* 16s* :: 2012/13 $16d^{bd}$ Aug 2 Won four times as a juvenile hurdler and picked up a race on the Flat before being brought down early on in the Galway Hurdle. There are a couple of four-year-old only races early in the season that could be an option, but I think he is going to want two and a half miles anyway, so there are no great plans for him at the moment. We will see how we go, but he could certainly be an interesting horse for the winter.

Hollow Tree (h137) 4 b.g Beat Hollow – Hesperia (Slip Anchor) 2011/12 17g* $16d^{2}$ 16v* 16v* $17d^{3}$ 17g Mar 16 Ran some cracking races last season, including when beating subsequent Triumph Hurdle winner Countrywide Flame in the Grade 1 at Chepstow over Christmas. He was in front turning for home at Cheltenham, but was just done for finishing speed. We will be looking to step him up in trip this season, to two and a half or even three miles. In hindsight, I probably should have run him in the two and a half mile novice at Cheltenham, but it is a difficult thing to do with a juvenile when there are two races for them already.

Bourne (h135) 6 gr.g Linamix (Fr) – L'Affaire Monique (Machiavellian (USA)) 2011/12 19s* $16d^{3}$ $16v^{2}$ 19d* 20g 20d $19s^{6}$ Apr 28 He's a very solid horse to run in those big two-and-a-half-mile handicap hurdles, although he might get a little bit further. He's not the biggest or most robust and I think he needs things to go his own way a bit, but there is certainly one of them in him as he has plenty of ability. He's back now, cantering away, and he's grand. Where he starts has yet to be decided, but he might need a couple of runs to get back in the swing of things.

Any Given Day (Ire) (h158) 7 gr.g Clodovil (Ire) – Five of Wands (Caerleon (USA)) 2011/12 20d* $20g^{4}$ Dec 10 He's not back in yet having had a setback, but he is due in shortly and will be running in two-and-a-half-mile conditions hurdles such as the Relkeel. He won a handicap at Haydock first time up last year, but that rather scuppered him for the rest of the season.

Ubaltique (Fr) (h132p) 4 b.g Balko (Fr) – Ode Antique (Fr) (Subotica (Fr)) 2011/12 17s* 18d5 16s* Apr 26 When we bought him from France he had already won, and after a run in the Grade 2 at Kelso he scored on his second start for us at Perth in April. He wasn't yet four when he won at Perth, and over the summer he has done really well. I don't think he's a star, but he's not badly handicapped. He's a likeable horse with a nice attitude.

Absinthe (Ire) (h130) 6 b.g King's Best (USA) – Triple Try (Ire) (Sadler's Wells (USA)) 2011/12 17s* 16d2 16s3 16d4 16g* :: 2012/13 17s* 17g4 16s2 Aug 18 Was previously with Walter Swinburn who also trained Overturn, and he has won twice for us, including on the Flat at Chester. We will stick to two-mile handicap hurdles with him and he should pay his way.

King's Grace (h123p) 6 b.g King's Theatre (Ire) – Beauchamp Grace (Ardross) 2011/12 16s6 20s* Dec 19 He could be very useful. He's had a couple of problems since winning at Bangor in December, but he's fine now and is cantering away. However, having won his novice, we are forced to go into handicaps or to go chasing. He is every inch a novice chaser, he's a gorgeous horse, but he has no experience. I don't really want to run him in handicap hurdles, because he is not a handicap hurdler, so where we go I don't really know, but he's got a lot of ability.

Halogen (h118p) 3 b.g Halling (USA) – Trompette (USA) (Bahri (USA)) 2012/13 17s* 17m* Aug 3 Had just the one run on the Flat as he had problems with the stalls, but he is a well-bred horse who has really taken to jumping, and should continue to do well in juvenile hurdles.

Novice Hurdlers

Tarlan (Ire) (h112p) 6 b.g Milan – Nethertara (Netherkelly) 2011/12 22d2 Nov 5 A lovely horse who should do well in novice hurdles. He probably should have won at Kelso on his debut for us last November, but he idled once hitting the front. He hasn't run since, as he sustained a small fracture at the top of his cannon bone. It might not have been the worst thing in the world as he is a big horse, a real staying chaser, and the time off has done him good.

Ifyousayso (Ire) (F101) 5 ch.g Definite Article – Rosato (Ire) (Roselier (Fr)) 2011/12 F16d* F17g* F17d5 Apr 14 I think he could be quite good. He won his first two starts and then was fifth in the big bumper at Aintree where Adrian (Lane) struggled to pull him up, he just kept galloping. I think he will want three miles and nice ground, but he could be a useful staying novice hurdler.

Howaboutnow (Ire) (F107) 5 ch.g Shantou (USA) – Sarah's Cottage (Ire) (Topanoora) 2011/12 F17v* F16s^{2} F17s* F17d Apr 14 I was a little disappointed with him at Aintree where he finished down the field in the bumper, behind Ifyousayso, but he was weak last year and is much stronger now. He is a full-brother to Super Duty, and whilst I don't think he is necessarily as good as his brother, he is certainly more than capable of winning two or three novices in the North.

Doyly Carte (F94) 4 b.f Doyen (Ire) – Generous Diana (Generous (Ire)) 2011/12 F16d* F16s^{2} F17d Apr 13 She is a half-sister to the smart Flat horse Dandino, and was very impressive winning her bumper at Catterick first time out. She was then beaten on bad ground at Kelso and was a little flat, so we waited for Aintree, but it just didn't happen there for her in what was a rough race. A good summer should have made a big difference to her as she is a huge filly.

Chasers

Weird Al (Ire) (c164) 9 b.g Accordion – Bucks Gift (Ire) (Buckley) 2011/12 c25d* c24d^{3} c26g^{pu} c36g^{F} Apr 14 He will go back to the Charlie Hall in an attempt to repeat his success of last year. He's not had a proper summer holiday as it took him a long time to get over the injury he sustained in the Grand National, where he took the skin off his fore-leg standing on himself when coming down at the fourth last. It was superficial, but it was pretty severe and there were lots of stitches. He's back in now and not been showing any ill effects, you can barely notice it, so he will go straight for the Charlie Hall. He has bled on occasions and I have a bit of a theory with him, in that it is stress related. He was in great nick before Cheltenham, but in the pre-parade ring, with the crowd and all the attention around Kauto Star you could see him getting physically tighter, and by the time he got onto the track he was cooked. It might be nonsense, but that was the impression I got, so we put a pair of earplugs on him in the National and tried our best to keep him as cool as possible. I think he took to Aintree, he jumped really well prior to coming down, but we've not really discussed plans for the second half of the season at this stage. He is very talented, but whether he is quite a Gold Cup horse I'm not so sure. We just have to mind him.

Ballabriggs (Ire) (c159) 11 b.g Presenting – Papoose (Ire) (Little Bighorn) 2011/12 c22d^{4} c36g^{6} Apr 14 We will kick on a bit more with him this year, there is nothing to lose now in terms of his handicap mark, although where we start I don't know. At this stage the Becher or Betfair Chase are two potential options we are looking at. He ran a blinder in the National again this year considering how worked up he got at the start. For a horse that is as switched off as he is, and he is one of the coolest horses I have ever seen, he got in a terrible state with the mess that went on. The stopping and starting, with the jockeys not being able to get off them because they didn't know what was happening really affected him. I've never seen him get like that. He didn't get away great, and I think it certainly cost him a top-four finish.

Our Mick (c147) 6 gr.g Karinga Bay – Dawn's Della (Scottish Reel) 2011/12 c16s^5 c16d^3 c19m* c20g* c20v* c20g^3 c24g^3 Mar 13 He's a fair tool. It took a while to convince the owner to let me run him over three miles and I don't think we went to Cheltenham that well handicapped, we were just short of places to go with him having won three races earlier in the campaign. I think he nearly could have won there though, he just missed one coming down the hill second time, and was a bit careful over the next couple before missing the last when he was staying on. I guess he has the profile of a Hennessy horse, but we will see.

Wymott (Ire) (c138§) 8 b.g Witness Box (USA) – Tanya Thyne (Ire) (Good Thyne (USA)) 2011/12 c26g^6 c24v^{pu} c24d^6 c24g Jan 28 He ran a great Grand National trial in the Hennessy last year on his reappearance, but he had a hard race there and had a setback later on, so he didn't see his season out. I guess you have to say he's a bit soft, and we've tried him in some headgear, but I certainly think he would jump around Aintree. He is owned by Trevor Hemmings so I would imagine he would be going to Aintree, either in the autumn or the spring, or both. He's a horse with plenty of ability, but we might just try and start him somewhere a little quieter to give him a confidence boost.

Tornado Bob (Ire) (h140 c?) 7 b.g Bob Back (USA) – Double Glazed (Ire) (Glacial Storm (USA)) 2011/12 c22d^F c20s^5 c24v^{pu} aF16d^2 24v 20g 21m^3 :: 2012/13 20d^6 May 18 Was one of our leading hopes for novice chases last year, but he completely lost his bottle after falling on chase debut. He has gone hunting for a bit before he comes back to me, and we will just play it by ear.

Across The Bay (Ire) (h138 c137) 8 b.g Bob's Return (Ire) – The Southern (Ire) (Glacial Storm (USA)) 2011/12 22g 24m 24g^2 24d^4 20v^2 24d^5 24g^{pu} 24d^3 Apr 12 He's going back over fences. He ran some good races over hurdles last year in contests he couldn't win, particularly when third to Big Buck's at Aintree. I thought he would run well in the Pertemps, but he seems to prefer smaller fields. He goes on slow ground and wants three miles plus. We haven't schooled him over fences, but he was a winner of a maiden chase in Ireland and he should make into a nice staying handicapper.

My Flora (c122) 8 b.m Alflora (Ire) – Bishop's Folly (Weld) 2011/12 c24g* c28g* c22d^F c26g^4 c20g* c23s* :: 2012/13 c28g^5 Jun 1 She has not been with us long, but she had a big reputation around here as a point to pointer and did well in hunter chases last season, finishing fourth in the Foxhunters at Cheltenham. She is eight, but is still a novice over hurdles, and with the number of mares only races being increased, there will be plenty of opportunities for her.

Novice Chasers

Overturn (Ire) (h165) 8 b.g Barathea (Ire) – Kristal Bridge (Kris) 2011/12 16g* 19g* 16s* 17g^2 16g^3 16g^2 Mar 13 The plan is to send him over fences. He had a break since he ran at Royal Ascot, but he's back in and cantering again now. I've only schooled him the once over fences, but the signs were very good, and as soon as he's straight enough we will press on with him. He's always jumped a hurdle like it's a fence, you don't see him kicking too many out of the ground, so it was no surprise to see him school over fences the way he did. The only thing stopping you from going chasing is the fact that it is Overturn, he's finished runner-up in a Champion Hurdle and you wouldn't want to see anything happen to him, but he deserves his chance at it.

Super Duty (Ire) (h136+) 6 b.g Shantou (USA) – Sarah's Cottage (Ire) (Topanoora) 2011/12 19d* 20d* 20v^F 19d* 20d^2 Apr 14 A horse who was purchased by my father, and he goes novice chasing. I haven't schooled him yet, but I think he could be very good. We were never going to beat Simonsig at Aintree, but I would have loved to have seen what would have happened had he not blundered at the second last. He was hating the ground (heavy) the day he fell at Ayr, though I still think he would have won had he stood up, so it was nice to see him on better ground at Aintree. He's a funny horse, very on-and-off the bridle, looking round all the time, playing at the job

Overturn winning the Fighting Fifth Hurdle at Newcastle

a little, like when he won at Ascot, though once Sam Thomas got stuck into him that day he galloped all the way home. I think he's very good, I just hope he jumps a fence.

Real Milan (Ire) (h136p) 7 b.g Milan – The Real Athlete (Ire) (Presenting) 2011/12 20s* 20v* 24v^{4} Feb 18 A lovely horse for staying novice chases. He won his first two starts for us over hurdles last year, and I think taking on Brindisi Breeze cost us second at Haydock. I thought he ran with great credit on that occasion, as from the moment he jumped off he wasn't enjoying the heavy ground. He could be a very nice horse.

Koup de Kanon (Fr) (126) 6 b.g Robin des Pres (Fr) – Coup de Sabre (Fr) (Sabrehill (USA)) 2011/12 17d* 19g^{5} 16v^{pu} 19s* 17d^{5} 16d Feb 11 He surprised me at times last season, especially with how well he travelled when runner-up at Cheltenham in January. He had a setback in the spring so he's not back here yet. He's got a bit more road work to do before he comes in, and when he does I would imagine we will go novice chasing. We will just tip away quietly with him.

Golden Call (Ire) (h137 c131p) 8 b.g Goldmark (USA) – Call Me Countess (Ire) (Aristocracy) 2011/12 F18g* F20d^{2} 20d^{3} 22s^{2} 24g* 25s^{4} aF16d^{4} 24g* 24g* 24d^{F} 24s^{2} :: 2012/13 c20s* May 19 I was very disappointed when he fell in the Grade 1 over hurdles at Aintree, as I thought he would love the place and run really well. He is quite old for a novice chaser, but he jumped really well when winning at Perth at the first time of asking. We've not got to the bottom of him yet so we don't know how good he is, that's what I wanted to find out at Aintree. I could see him ending up in the four-miler at Cheltenham.

Other horses of note

With the program of mares races ever expanding, you always wants a certain number in the yard, and two that should win plenty of races are **Diligent** who goes novice hurdling, and **She Ranks Me**. In terms of novice hurdlers, **Beeves**, **Grouse Lodge** and **Mulligan's Man** are all already winners and have similar profiles. They might not be top-class, but they are tough, going to stay, will jump a fence and win plenty of races. In the novice chase ranks, a couple which deserve a mention are **Diocles** and **Sydney Paget** who should both progress into very nice staying prospects. I've also got a massive bunch from Irish points, including **Clondaw Kaempfer** who won the big sales bumper at Fairyhouse in April, **Clondaw Draft**, **Oscatara** who is a half-brother to Tarlan, **Up And Go**, **Dreams of Milan**, and **Blackwater King** to name just a few. They are the ones I get excited about because you don't really know how good they are going to be.

FUTURE STARS

John Ferguson

Name	**JOHN FERGUSON**
Base	Newmarket, Suffolk
First Full Licence	2011
First Jumps Winner	Cape Dutch, Hexham, 30/09/11
Total Winners	25
Best Horse Trained	Cotton Mill (Timeform rating h146)

Many people would jump at the chance for some jet-setting to escape a British winter, but John Ferguson has decided to forego the hospitality on offer at Meydan, Santa Anita and Sha Tin so that he can instead brave the elements at rather less exotic venues such as Fakenham, Hereford and Plumpton. Ferguson's decision to scale back his prominent role in Sheikh Mohammed's Darley bloodstock empire in order to concentrate on a training

John Ferguson with stable star Cotton Mill

career may have resulted in the loss of some Air Miles, but he has had little cause to regret it otherwise. The stable's impressive haul of twenty-four wins during its first full campaign in 2011/12 was achieved at a strike rate of 31%—the best such statistic by a British-based trainer in the top hundred of the championship table, bettering even those posted by Nicholls (23%) and Henderson (27%). The self-effacing Ferguson has described his approach to training as "making it up as I go along", but his policy of exploiting well-bred horses (often expensive Darley cast-offs) who matured too slowly both physically and mentally to show their best on the Flat is clearly no accident. "My feeling is that whether jumping or on the Flat, a fast horse will always beat a slow horse. If a Flat-bred horse can settle, jump and stay then I'd have thought he'd beat one with a jumping pedigree", explains Ferguson. The theory has certainly worked out well so far, with the likes of New Year's Eve (who fetched 120,000 guineas as a yearling but didn't race on the Flat) and Cotton Mill (a lightly-raced winner on the Flat for William Jarvis) both figuring prominently for the stable at the Cheltenham Festival. Meanwhile, the exploits of pointer/hunter chaser Earth Dream, who has been rejuvenated since joining Ferguson from Paul Nicholls, illustrates that the yard's success isn't restricted to its Flat recruits. Although Ferguson's lucrative level-stakes profit returns are likely to subside as bookies and punters alike grow wise to his fledgling string, this remains a stable well worth following in 2012/13.

Trainer's Horse To Follow: I was very pleased with the performance of **Once More Dubai** when he won on his first start for us in September. I plan to run him at Kempton on 21st October. He seems to have enjoyed his outing at Plumpton and I hope he can give us some fun.

Richard Woollacott

Name	RICHARD WOOLLACOTT
Base	South Molton, Devon
First Full Licence	2012
First Jumps Winner	Parkam Jack, Worcester, 20/06/12
Total Winners	11
Best Horse Trained	Gay Sloane (Timeform Rating h126+)

Professional sport is littered with examples of "future stars" who fail to fulfil their early promise—for example, precocious teenager Danny Cadamarteri looked destined for the top when scoring five goals (including the winner in a Merseyside derby) in his first seven games for Everton but was turning out for Grays Athletic less than ten years later. Hopefully, rookie trainer Richard Woollacott will enjoy a career path more in the mould of another product of Everton's youth team, Wayne Rooney, after making a similarly successful start when taking on the big boys. A prolific winner in points, both as a jockey and trainer, Woollacott has made a big impact since taking out a professional licence this summer—it took less than two months for his wins tally to reach double figures, with an impressive strike rate (29%) and level-stakes profit (£16) to match. Those winners have been a combination of unexposed sorts from the pointing ranks and, more significantly, cheap recruits from other yards who've been rejuvenated by the switch to Woollacott's regime. The latter group includes the prolific Allerford Jack, who hasn't looked back (including in points) since joining the yard from Caroline Keevil after the end of 2010/11, whilst Charlie Mann and Andy Turnell are others who've witnessed hitherto difficult-to-win-with former charges of theirs register victories for Woollacott this summer. Of course, Woollacott will probably struggle to find sufficient ammunition to maintain that impressive strike rate as racing gets more competitive over the winter months, but it is worth noting that the likes of Evan Williams and Tim Vaughan both made their mark on the summer jumping scene before becoming established top ten trainers in recent seasons. The early signs suggest that the ambitious Woollacott could make similar strides sooner rather than later.

Trainer's Horse To Follow: **Civil Disobedience**, who we've acquired from Caroline Keevil, is a novice chaser we like as he had some good form in point-to-points, where he was unbeaten in four starts. He was going really well until falling two out at Warwick on his penultimate start and we'd like to think he can be very competitive in some reasonable staying chases (half-brother to fairly useful staying chaser Drybrook Bedouin).

Jamie Snowden

Name	**JAMIE SNOWDEN**
Base	Lambourn, Berkshire
First Full Licence	2008
First Jumps Winner	Marsh Court, Fontwell, 4/10/08
Total Winners	40
Best Horse Trained	Marodima (Timeform Rating c140)

In contrast to John Ferguson and Richard Woollacott, Jamie Snowden certainly didn't hit the ground running upon taking out his training licence in 2008/9—wins proved to be hard to come by in each of his first three campaigns, with a paltry strike rate ranging from 4% to 7% during that period. A switch to Lambourn last summer, however, has coincided with a marked upturn in fortunes for Snowden, who now seems to be making up for lost time with a vengeance. Strike rate was up to a much more respectable 16% in 2011/12, whilst there were also significant increases in terms of both wins and prize money. Veteran chaser Knighton Combe was the biggest contributor in the latter category (thanks largely to his win in the Summer National at Uttoxeter), though Snowden's handling of the seemingly-exposed Marodima (claimed by him for £12,000 in early-2010/11) was arguably the greater achievement—the yard conjured three wins out of the headstrong front runner in 2011/12, which was by far his most consistent campaign in a long while. Encouragingly, the early months of 2012/13 suggest that last season's achievements won't prove to be a one-off for Snowden, who will clearly have learned a thing or two during his spell as assistant trainer to Nicky Henderson. Indeed, it wouldn't be the biggest surprise if he followed in the footsteps of another former Henderson assistant Charlie Longsdon, who endured a very disappointing 2009/10 campaign (strike rate of just 7%) but has flourished in both subsequent seasons and could boast the fifth best strike rate (20%) inside the top thirty of the latest championship table.

Trainer's Horse To Follow: A horse to follow for the season—we have a couple of interesting horses—but I would have to say **Present View**. He is a gorgeous-looking four-year-old by Presenting who ran in two Irish Points. He fell two out on his first start at Dromahane when looking likely to win, but he made amends at Lismore the following week when bolting up. He will start off in a novice hurdle at Kempton in late October, and could be exciting for the years to come especially when sent chasing. Another of interest is a mare called **Magic Vixen**—she is a five-year-old by Old Vic, and is a three-parts sister to Kicking King. She won a bumper at Limerick and looks a serious horse for novice hurdles this season.

Tom Cannon

Name	**TOM CANNON**
Attached Stable	Chris Gordon
First Ride	15/05/08
First Winner	Days of Pleasure, Fontwell, 10/03/10
Total Winners	53
Best Horse Ridden	Starluck (Timeform Rating h155)

It can be hard for promising conditional jockeys to get noticed if they're not attached to a big yard, both in terms of big-race opportunities and outside rides. A case in point is Tom Cannon, who appeals to us as just about the most complete jockey amongst the current crop of conditionals, yet is still operating below the radar somewhat—despite briefly becoming a YouTube hit late last season for his acrobatic recovery from a bad mistake when winning aboard Inthejungle at Plumpton in April. As that venue would suggest,

Cannon is largely plying his trade at some of jumping's lower-profile tracks at present (he has particularly good records at Folkestone and Fontwell), but if the right breaks go his way, then there is no reason why he shouldn't be showing off his talents on a bigger stage soon. With a background in pony racing, show jumping and eventing, Cannon's remarkable display of horsemanship in that aforementioned clip arguably shouldn't come as a surprise, though it should also be noted that he has also displayed plenty of race-craft to date. Indeed, he already has plenty of commendable never-say-die efforts from the saddle on his CV but, unlike many young jockeys, hasn't been overdependent on the whip to do so. Cannon's emergence last season coincided with a career-best campaign for Hampshire-based trainer Chris Gordon, who currently provides the jockey (now claiming 3 lb) with the bulk of his rides. With outside rides starting to come in from the likes of Nick Gifford, Lawney Hill and David Bridgwater, it is to be hoped Cannon will raise his profile a bit more in 2012/13.

Brendan Powell Jr

Name	**BRENDAN POWELL JR**
Attached Stable	Colin Tizzard
First Ride	4/02/11
First Winner	Home, Southwell, 8/02/11
Total Winners	42
Best Horse Ridden	Oiseau de Nuit (Timeform Rating c151)

Brendan Powell Jr

Nepotism has long been rife in sport, none more so than in racing. For example, regardless of which side you sit on the debate about the merit of the ride given to Camelot when failing to complete the Triple Crown in the St Leger this autumn, there can be little doubt that Joseph O'Brien wouldn't have been fast-tracked to the plum job of stable jockey at Ballydoyle had he not been the trainer's son. The flip side to such scenarios, of course, is that people born into racing families are bred for the job in every sense of that phrase. Brendan Powell Jr certainly falls into this category and, although sharing the name of his Grand National-winning dad has clearly helped him getting noticed, the teenager has already shown enough in the saddle to suggest he'd be making waves even without such outside help, his impressive haul of winners in 2011/12 including a treble at Plumpton in December. The 3-lb claimer scores heavily for stylishness in the saddle, with the fact he's light enough to also ride on the Flat almost certainly helping in that regard, whilst a grounding in the ultra-competitive field of Irish pony racing means he's rarely found wanting in a finish either. Powell Sr, understandably, has provided his son with the bulk of his rides so far and that link-up coincided with the Upper Lambourn trainer enjoying his best campaign for several years. However, it is Powell Jr's association with Colin Tizzard (who supplied two of those Plumpton winners) which could prove to be the most fruitful looking further ahead, particularly as that yard's own father-son set-up presumably won't carry on for all that much longer now that Joe Tizzard is well into his thirties. Powell has already caught the eye when replacing the latter in the saddle on several occasions so far, particularly in conjuring back-to-form performances from some of the yard's unreliable chasers. Indeed, Powell seems to have that invaluable knack of getting horses to run and jump for him, so the future is clearly bright if he can steer clear of serious injury over the next few years.

ANTE-POST BETTING

"You've got to speculate to accumulate" is the kind of hackneyed expression often trotted out by wannabe businessmen, admittedly by those more in the mould of Del Boy than Sir Richard Branson. In truth, this proverb holds little truth in many financial matters and usually represents nothing more than an invitation to gamble blindly rather than actual advice. Take ante-post betting, for example, which offers punters scant value in cramped markets that are stacked very much in favour of the bookmakers, particularly as history suggests only a fraction of the runners will even make it to the starting line (all money is lost on non-runners, of course). Indeed, punters are often better off keeping their powder dry until nearer the time, both in terms of the odds on offer and reducing the risk of non-runners. There are exceptions to that rule, however, as Conor Murphy demonstrated with his memorable £1million windfall at the latest Cheltenham Festival. The then-Nicky Henderson stable lad reaped the benefits of placing a £50 accumulator on five of the yard's best horses fully four months before the Festival itself. Had Murphy waited until the Festival to place his bet at SP odds, he'd have won just over £32,000—a handy total, but not the sort of life-changing amount which helped fund Murphy's emigration to the USA this summer, where he plans to set himself up as a trainer in Kentucky. As it was, the autumn odds secured on Sprinter Sacre (6/1), Simonsig (12/1), Bobs Worth (6/1), Finian's Rainbow (8/1) and Riverside Theatre (10/1) netted him considerably more than that—the accumulator would have actually paid over £3million but for the seven-figure payment limit in place by Murphy's bookmaker. For the record, Bobs Worth and Finian's Rainbow were both recommended at 10/1 in these pages last year, but space constraints must have prevented us from tipping the other three names (no doubt at bigger odds too) to complete the same five-timer!

In fairness, the risks involved in ante-post betting have reduced somewhat since the advent of Betfair, with punters now able to lay bets off to cover the eventuality of any possible non-runners. Nevertheless, there still isn't much scope for manoeuvre when dealing with those towards the head of the ante-post markets—for example, the current best ante-post odds on Sprinter Sacre (5/4) and Big Buck's (6/4), for the Queen Mother Champion Chase and World Hurdle respectably, are unlikely to change much until nearer the time of those races, so there is little point wading in at those sort of odds six months beforehand if the tag "with a run" isn't attached. Therefore, it is preferable to seek out a few longer shots whose odds are likely to shorten markedly over the winter months as they emerge as a serious contender for their big-race targets.

As usual, there are major fluctuations between the ante-post markets for the two major championships for staying chasers, namely Kempton's King George VI Chase on Boxing Day and the Cheltenham Gold Cup in March. For example, David Pipe's second-season chaser

Grands Crus is 6/1 second favourite for Kempton, as opposed to the seventh choice at 20/1 for Cheltenham, with the different nature of those two tracks (and to a lesser extent the different trips) the main reason for such a disparity. Previous winner Long Run still sets a high standard despite having to settle for minor honours at both Kempton and Cheltenham last season, though his odds do look on the cramped side for the festive showpiece, particularly as there are three potential serious rivals from within his own stable—namely Conor Murphy's old friends Bobs Worth (not a certain runner), Riverside Theatre (runner-up to Long Run in 2010/11) and Finian's Rainbow. Of that trio, Finian's Rainbow makes the most appeal at 8/1, even though he's still got stamina to prove at the longer trip. However, it could pay to side with the Paul Nicholls stable as it searches for a replacement to five-times winner Kauto Star. Silviniaco Conti is probably overpriced at 14/1, though connections are reportedly planning a relatively quiet campaign for him (he's due to miss Cheltenham again in favour of Aintree). By contrast, Kempton has long been the target for fellow second-season chaser **Al Ferof**—indeed, Ruby Walsh's first words to owner John Hales after the gelding had finished third in the Victor Chandler Chase at Ascot last winter were "what a ride he'd be in the King George next season". Admittedly, Al Ferof's novice chase campaign did end in something of an anti-climax when disappointing at both Cheltenham (let down by a rare jumping error) and Aintree (shaped as if over the top), but he'd seemed destined for big things prior to that and looks each-way value at 20/1 for the King George, particularly as the step-up in trip has long seemed likely to suit.

Sir des Champs will be bidding to make it three wins at the Festival next March

There are plenty of valuable alternatives on home soil for leading Irish-trained chasers during the first two-thirds of the season, but there are no such distractions come Cheltenham in March. **Sir des Champs** numbers wins at the last two Festivals amongst his unbeaten run of seven since joining the all-conquering yard of Willie Mullins and is already favourite to complete a notable hat-trick in the blue riband event itself, the Cheltenham Gold Cup. That said, the 6/1 currently available about him could soon look very big if he extends that winning sequence further over the coming months, which seems likely given he'll probably be tackling small-field events on Irish soil to begin with. We've long since nailed our colours to Sir des Champs as one likely to go to the very top and are not about to desert him now! It may be premature to desert **Long Run** too. Admittedly, Long Run goes into the 2012/13 campaign with a bit to prove following his below-par third at Cheltenham in March, whilst the historical stats are rather stacked against him—Kauto Star is the only Gold Cup winner to regain his title. That said, he remains the highest-rated horse from last season quoted in the ante-post lists for the race, so best odds of 8/1 must be considered too big, particularly given his largely consistent profile at this level.

Consistency has also been the strong suit of **Finian's Rainbow**, having won seven of his nine starts (runner-up in Grade 1 company on the other two) over fences to date. As has already been alluded to, he is set to tackle three miles for the first time in the King George, but will almost certainly revert to shorter for his Cheltenham Festival target. With his outstanding stable-companion Sprinter Sacre standing in the way should he defend his crown in the Queen Mother Champion Chase, a switch to the intermediate trip on offer in the Ryanair Chase makes plenty of sense. A smooth win over two and a half miles at Aintree in April suggests Finian's Rainbow won't have any problems with the Ryanair trip and, currently trading at around 7/1, he certainly makes more appeal than 2012 winner Riverside Theatre in the ante-post market. Another of last season's Festival winners who may end up in the Ryanair is **Salut Flo**. He ran out an impressive winner of the Byrne Group Plate and may yet have more to offer after just four starts for present connections since arriving from France. Given the Pipe family's strong tradition in the Paddy Power Gold Cup, Salut Flo will presumably have that valuable prize as his autumn target and, provided all goes well there, a switch to graded company could well be on the cards later in the campaign—he therefore looks a sporting punt at 25/1 in the Ryanair market.

One horse who's already proved himself at graded level after tackling valuable handicap company is **Darlan**, who showed no ill-effects from a heavy fall at the second last (when still holding every chance) in the Betfair Hurdle at Newbury when going on to perform with credit at both Cheltenham and Aintree later in 2011/12. Arguably unlucky when runner-up to Cinders And Ashes in the Supreme Novices'at Cheltenham, Darlan then created a very good impression when leading home a Nicky Henderson one-two-four in the Top Novices' at Aintree. Henderson could well have another embarrassment of riches come the Champion Hurdle next March—he's currently responsible for six of the first 10 in the ante-post betting for the race—and the chances are Darlan will find the necessary improvement to figure prominently in the pecking order at Seven Barrows by then. He's certainly a more attractive proposition at this stage than the same owner's 2010 winner Binocular, whilst the likes of Simonsig and Oscar Whisky also have the option of chasing in 2012/13. Reigning champion Rock On Ruby, of course, helped Paul Nicholls to edge out Henderson in the latest trainers' championship, though he'll have a new handler when defending his crown following the decision to send him to rookie trainer Harry Fry. In truth, Fry was the man in charge last season too (he operated a satellite yard for Nicholls) and a bigger concern is the fact Rock On Ruby came up short in Grade 1 company either side of his Cheltenham win. Indeed, the Hurricane Fly of 2011 would be the one to beat amongst the established order in the two-mile hurdling division, though 5/1 is no value about a horse who has twice missed the Festival through injury.

If we're talking about high-risk betting strategies, then backing the ante-post favourite for a championship novice chase without having seen him or her jump a fence in public must be up there amongst the worst. However, **Boston Bob** looks tailor-made for the RSA Chase and is worth siding with at 10/1 despite those reservations. For a start, he already has some chasing experience courtesy of his debut win in an Irish maiden point in 2010 (when defeating subsequent Grade 2-winning novice chaser Days Hotel) prior to his big-money purchase by Graham and Andrea Wylie. Boston Bob quickly developed into a very smart hurdler following his switch to Willie Mullins last summer, winning his first three starts (including twice in graded company) before finishing runner-up to the ill-fated Brindisi

Prince de Beauchene will probably have a campaign geared around the Grand National

Breeze when favourite for the Spa Hurdle at Cheltenham. Expect him to run up a similar sequence in novice chases on home soil before a return trip to Prestbury Park next March, when we expect him to hold strong claims of going one better than in 2012.

The Wylies have enjoyed plenty of success with the handful of horses they sent to Mullins following the disqualification of their former trainer Howard Johnson. Two of their Mullins team, **On His Own** and **Prince de Beauchene**, quickly developed into live Grand National contenders during the latest campaign and must be at the top of any shortlist for the 2013 edition, for which they are both currently trading at a best price of 25/1. On His Own was travelling as well as anything when falling at second Becher's (had looked a natural over the fences until then) and holds strong claims of emulating West Tip, who returned from a tumble there when going best in 1985 to win twelve months later. Prince de Beauchene would have been the Wylie first string (and likely hot favourite) at Aintree but for missing the race due to a late injury setback. He'll be much higher in the weights in 2013 but is still worthy of serious consideration having looked a much improved performer in just two starts so far for Mullins. Fluent jumping and prominent tactics are usually a potent combination over the National fences, so the 33/1 on offer about National Hunt Chase winner **Teaforthree** is also very tempting, particularly as that race has proved an increasingly good trial for the main Nationals in recent years. Rebecca Curtis has already earmarked the Aintree showpiece as his target and, as a result, he could well have a campaign geared around protecting the gelding's handicap mark. Now that we've identified the first three for next year's National, all you've got to do is find a bookmaker willing to price up a tricast for them in the race—then you may be able to secure a payout similar to that of the USA's newest resident Conor Murphy . . .

Ante-Post Selections

Al Ferof
King George VI Chase (20/1 e-w)

Darlan
Champion Hurdle (14/1)

Boston Bob
RSA Chase (10/1)

Finian's Rainbow
Ryanair Chase (7/1)

Salut Flo
Ryanair Chase (25/1 e-w)

Sir des Champs
Cheltenham Gold Cup (6/1)

Long Run
Cheltenham Gold Cup (8/1)

On His Own
Grand National (25/1)

Prince de Beauchene
Grand National (25/1)

Teaforthree
Grand National (33/1)

THE CHIEF CORRESPONDENT

Will Hurricane fly? Will Kauto star? Will Long or Albertas run? Will The Giant bolster? Will Imperial command? Er, who knows, but these are all key questions that need to be asked of the established chasers and hurdlers ahead of what could be a pivotal jumps season: out with the old and in with the new. On January 1st this year, the odds of the holders defending their championship titles at Cheltenham–namely Long Run, Hurricane Fly, Sizing Europe and Big Buck's–were only 9/4, 2/1, 5/2 and 1/2 respectively. Looking towards Cheltenham 2013, the accumulative odds for the defenders, sadly a back three than back four this time after Synchronised's death, is approximately 200/1, and that's with Big Buck's at 6/4.

The point is that, Big Buck's apart, there's not so much a wind of change as a great big tornado, especially in the chasing division, where Sprinter Sacre already has three hooves on the Champion Chase trophy and Sir des Champs looks to have at least a frog on the Gold Cup. Neither has been missed in the ante-post betting, though, and the better value is often found in combing the more obscure and exotic markets* for the 2012/13 National Hunt season. So, let's do exactly that.

*(*not all of these forecasts or indeed markets may be 100% legitimate)*

ODDS: 4/9 Henderson, 2/1 Nicholls, 12/1 McCain
MARKET: Champion Trainer (by the way, Henderson should be 1/9 and not 4/9)

ODDS: N/O Henderson, N/O Nicholls, N/O McCain
MARKET: Who is privately still desperate to get his hands on Somersby, oddly now with Flat trainer Mick Channon after the retirement of the Hen?

*To follow Timeform's Chief Correspondent Jamie Lynch through the season, visit: **betting.betfair.com/horse-racing/timeform-features/jamie-lynch***

ODDS: 8/1 Rhyll, 11/1 Baghdad, 25/1 Chernobyl

MARKET: Following on from the likes of Europe, Australia and Santiago, what will be the suffix of the next in the series of 'Sizing' horses?

ODDS: 8/1 Rhyll, 11/1 Baghdad, 25/1 Chernobyl

MARKET: The next venue to announce a Cheltenham Preview night.

ODDS: 4/5 the Cider Museum, 7/4 the cattle market, 10/3 Beryl Reid's birthplace

MARKET: What will become the new number one visitor attraction in Hereford?

ODDS: 8/15 ten minutes but don't tell anyone, 9/2 24-48 hours, 7/1 over 48 hours

MARKET: How long will it take Phil Smith to tinker with and frame the Grand National weights?

ODDS: 7/4 Mouse, 10/3 Badger, 4/1 Shark, 9/2 Hare

MARKET: Animal Magic – which of the animal nicknames will have the most wins this season; Mouse (Morris, Irish trainer), Badger (McAlister, Scottish jockey), Shark (Hanlon, Irish trainer), Timmy Murphy.

ODDS: 9/4 table tennis championships, 7/1 table football championships, 9/1 Diagnosis Murder

MARKET: What the BBC will be showing on the afternoon of the Grand National.

ODDS: 1/1,000,000 none, 1,000,000/1 one, 1,000,000/1 two

MARKET: How many times will Quevega run before winning at Cheltenam, OR, how many times will Big Buck's be beaten, OR, what's the percentage chance of Tony McCoy not winning an eighteenth successive jockeys' championship, OR, the positive difference the BHA's new novice chase rule will make, OR, how many hurdle races will be staged at Chester.

And finally, with some worthwhile advice included, a poem, entitled:

Oh My Darlan Cheltenham-time

So it's out with the old and in with the new,
Time's up for Kauto, the time's now for Grands Crus.
Time's up for Long Run who looks past his pomp,
There's a new gang in town, led by Sir des Champs.
Same goes for two-milers in expert opinions,
Say bye bye to Sizing, to Big Zeb and Finian's,
Each was a blessing but none have a prayer
Up against Sprinter Sacre, or even Sanctuaire.
But some never change; Big Mac's clothes or his girdle,
Or a flat spot for Big Buck's as he wins the World Hurdle.
But enough of this nonsense and trying to be funny,
What's the one bet to have that will win us big money?
It comes in the Champion, the Hurdle not Chase,
And to keep with the theme, his is a new(ish) face.
So get on him now, before J. P. if you can,
It's his horse we're backing, up-and-comer Darlan.
But we learn from the past, and the single best bet
Is to keep an eye in-running on Voler La Vedette.

SECTION 4

TIMEFORM'S VIEW

Chosen from the Timeform Formbook, here is Timeform's detailed analysis—compiled by our team of race reporters and supplemented by observations from Timeform's handicappers—of a selection of key races from the 2011/12 British jumps season.

CHELTENHAM Saturday, Nov 12
GOOD to SOFT (Old Course)

2461 Paddy Power Gold Cup Chase (Hcap) (Gr 3) (1) (170) (4yo+) £85,425 — 2½m110y (16)

Last run	Horse / Trainer / Age-Weight / Jockey	SP	Dist	Pos
4601^{6}	GREAT ENDEAVOUR (IRE) *DavidPipe* 7-10-3^{147} TimmyMurphy	10 8/1		1
76	QUANTITATIVEEASING (IRE) *NickyHenderson* 6-10-0^{144} AndrewTinkler	20/1	7	2
2215^{pu}	DIVERS (FR) *FerdyMurphy* 7-10-0^{144} GrahamLee	20/1	3½	3
4628^{2}	AERIAL (FR) *PaulNicholls* 5-9-11^{144} RyanMahon^{3}	33/1	4½	4
1988^{*}	Billie Magern *NigelTwiston-Davies* 7-10-0^{144} SamTwiston-Davies	20/1	13	5
275^{*}	Wishfull Thinking *PhilipHobbs* 8-11-6^{164} (t) RichardJohnson	5 7/2f	3¾	6
4587^{2}	Mon Parrain (FR) *PaulNicholls* 5-10-8^{152} RWalsh	9/2	½	7
4602^{f}	Calgary Bay (IRE) *HenriettaKnight* 8-10-2^{146} HaddenFrost	20/1	6	8
2090^{2}	Fine Parchment (IRE) *CharlieMann* 8-9-9^{144} (t) PeterCarberry^{5}	33/1	hd	9
2186^{2}	Araldur (FR) *AlanKing* 7-10-0^{144} RobertThornton	14 12/1	hd	10
2700	Dave's Dream (IRE) *NickyHenderson* 8-10-3^{147} (s) BarryGeraghty	9/1	1	11
2256^{3}	Oiseau de Nuit (FR) *ColinTizzard* 9-9-13^{153} BrendanPowell^{10}	33/1	5	12
1662^{*}	Finger Onthe Pulse (IRE) *TomJTaaffe,Ireland* 10-10-2^{146} (t) PaulCarberry	33/1	10	13
1904^{2}	Swincombe Rock *NigelTwiston-Davies* 6-10-0^{144} DavidEngland	40/1	½	14
1932^{2}	Loosen My Load (IRE) *HenrydeBromhead,Ireland* 7-10-9^{153} AELynch	16/1	2	15
4690^{2}	Holmwood Legend *KieranBurke* 10-10-3^{147} JohnnyFarrelly	33/1	5	16
2097^{5}	Tullamore Dew (IRE) *NickGifford* 9-10-0^{144} LiamTreadwell	20/1		f
2200^{5}	Poquelin (FR) *PaulNicholls* 8-11-5^{170} DavidPrichard^{7}	25/1		ur
2097^{4}	The Giant Bolster *DavidBridgwater* 6-10-2^{146} (s) TomScudamore	12 10/1		ur
1737^{ur}	Noble Alan (GER) *NickyRichards* 8-10-0^{144} DougieCostello	20/1		ur

2.35race Mr D. A. Johnson 20ran 5m01.50

On paper a really competitive renewal of one of the top handicaps of the whole season, but it was run at a searching gallop that few were comfortable with, the winner coping much better than his rivals with the way the race was run, while the placed horses belatedly boosted the form of the Centenary Novices' Handicap at the Festival in March. **Great Endeavour** is building a really good record in these big Cheltenham handicaps, adding to his success in the 2010 Plate, coping much better than his rivals with the searching gallop set and always well placed, in no danger after being sent on after 3 out, despite mistakes at the last 2 fences, galloping on strongly to the line; he was well treated on the best of his form and didn't need to improve much to land this, though he'll still look just about the pick of the weights in the Hennessy and ought to go close in that provided the race doesn't either come too soon or turn into too much of a slog at 3¼m. **Quantitativeeasing** emerged with plenty of credit on his first start out of novice company, not obviously fancied judged on the market for all he'd looked a likely sort for this race at the Festival here, travelling well waited with and finding plenty when let down, his jumping standing up well to the demands of the test save for an error 2 out; he's likely to stay a bit further, and as such will be of interest again in similar events, starting at the International meeting here next month. **Divers**, 5 lb out of the handicap, ran almost to the pound on revised terms with the runner-up from the Centenary Handicap at the Festival here, again coming from well back, not really making headway until 3 out, his effort just flattening out after the last; this suggests he'll be a factor in similar events again. **Aerial** had undergone a breathing operation since last seen back in April, and that was presumably a factor in this good effort, seeing the race out well after a mistake when still towards the rear at the eleventh; he was 4 lb out of the weights here and is likely to be competitive off his proper mark with this behind him. **Billie Magern** was off a mark 11 lb higher than last time (5 lb out of the weights) and finished about as high up the field as could be expected, the way in which he rallied after completely losing his position all to his credit. **Wishfull Thinking** was obviously below form on his first start since producing the best novice performance of the last campaign at Punchestown in May, that form having been franked subsequently, but the tactics were seriously overdone and he has to be worth another chance to confirm that effort, which suggests he'll be a place contender in some of the best races this season; he was restrained at the start but soon started pulling and had joined the leader by the third, forcing the pace even more soon after and clear jumping boldly through the middle of the race before he was headed after 3 out and had nothing left; he's been below form due to an aggressive ride on his last 2 appearances on this track, and it is just possible a flatter course will suit him better, despite last season's handicap win here. **Mon Parrain** looked an exciting prospect in 2 outings in Britain last season but was in nothing like the same form on his return, weak in the market on the day and barely ever looking at ease (jumped none too fluently), losing his position completely by the tenth before running past beaten horses late on; he's sufficiently unexposed to bounce back from this reverse. **Calgary Bay** just couldn't cope with the run of the race on his first start since falling early in the Grand National, making a mistake at the sixth and soon losing his position; he's become hard to win with anyhow. **Fine Parchment** raced close up for a long way, one of few comfortable with the pace mid-race and shaping as if still in form, but he was unable to quicken 3 out, his task from 6 lb out of the handicap plainly beyond him. **Araldur**'s jumping didn't hold up faced with this much more exacting test and he was beaten after mistakes at the eighth and eleventh, essentially running poorly. **Dave's Dream** has a good record fresh, but he's also presumably been hard to keep sound and, tried in cheekpieces, he found so little after appearing to be going well before 3 out that he might have had a physical problem, surely not undone totally for stamina at this trip for all he's yet to perform beyond 2m. **Oiseau de Nuit** was unlikely to be seen to advantage over this trip but his jumping let him down before lack of stamina came into play, a blunder at the eleventh when still going okay effectively ending his chance. **Finger Onthe Pulse** found this a much sterner test than a minor event in a small field and was nowhere near his best, soon unable to hold his early prominent position. **Swincombe Rock** was out of the weights and faced an inadequate test of stamina in a better race, duly struggling in rear by the seventh. **Loosen My Load**, sweating, has little chance off his current BHA mark in any sort of competitive event and he never figured, making a mistake at the fourth. **Holmwood Legend** is going to be really up against it in competitive handicaps off this sort of mark, his jumping just compounding his lack of competitiveness, on the retreat when making his third mistake of note 4 out. **Tullamore Dew** had still to be asked for his effort when he fell at the eleventh; the performances of the second and third suggest he's on a workable mark and likely to be of interest again. **Poquelin** was running respectably, keeping on while unlikely to trouble the principals, when he unseated 3 out; he has to be vulnerable in competitive races off his current mark, however. **The Giant Bolster**'s jumping isn't the best, though it was hardly an error that caused his rider to be unseated at the first. **Noble Alan** is becoming rather accident prone, though the way he was moving forward before blundering and unseating in spectacular fashion 4 out suggests he may well go close off his current mark if he can avoid the odd mistake.

HAYDOCK Saturday, Nov 19
GOOD to SOFT

2621 Betfair Chase (Lancashire) (Gr 1) (1) (5yo+) £113,072 3m (18)

235 pu	KAUTO STAR (FR) *PaulNicholls* 11-11-7 (t) RWalsh	11/2 6/1		1
*4253**	LONG RUN (FR) *NickyHenderson* 6-11-7 MrSWaley-Cohen	5/4 6/5f	8	2
2200*	WEIRD AL (IRE) *DonaldMcCain* 8-11-7 TimmyMurphy	6 7/1	2	3
*2674**	Diamond Harry *NickWilliams* 8-11-7 JamesReveley	4 7/2	8	4
2200 2	Time For Rupert (IRE) *PaulWebber* 7-11-7 WillKennedy	7 6/1	7	5
2087 2	Pure Faith (IRE) *PeterBowen* 7-11-7 TomO'Brien	66/1		pu

3.05race Mr Clive D. Smith 6ran 5m54.20

A top renewal of the Betfair Chase, attracting last season's King George and Gold Cup winner Long Run as well as Kauto Star, whilst Diamond Harry, Weird Al and Time For Rupert are all lightly-raced chasers who arrived with some untapped potential; admittedly, not all of them were primed for the day, but it was still an excellent effort from Kauto Star to win this race for the fourth time, the result a solid one on the day with the winner ensuring a good gallop. **Kauto Star** no longer seemed capable of such a top-notch performance but came back from 6½ months off with his best effort since the 2009 King George, gaining a remarkable fifteenth Grade 1 chase win in the process, and, although it's a little short in form terms of his outstanding best, to bounce back like this in the autumn of his career adds emphasis to the fact that Kauto Star is one of National Hunt's all-time greats; he was ridden differently to usual, forcing the pace with no obvious front runner in the field, and it was good to see him race so enthusiastically, jumping impeccably and lasting until 2 out on the bridle, then finding under pressure to see off the challenge of Long Run; it has to be said that Kauto Star was 100% prepared for the day, a point underlined by his trainer in the build up, and the feeling is that nowadays he needs more time between races than the 5 weeks before the King George. **Long Run**'s defeat isn't really a concern given his primary target is the King George and, unlike Kauto Star, he wasn't at concert pitch for this reappearance, still the one to beat at Kempton all things considered, but, unusually for a chaser of his calibre, Long Run's tendency to make mistakes does mean there's always a degree of risk attached in backing him, especially at short prices; this was a more than satisfactory reappearance on the figures, good enough in fact to win an average Betfair Chase, but his jumping wasn't totally convincing even before mistakes at the eleventh and thirteenth, under pressure not long after the latter but responding until lack of peak fitness appeared to tell before the last; he is a chaser of the highest order and will no doubt add to his haul of Grade 1 wins. **Weird Al** had much stiffer competition than in the Charlie Hall, up against Kauto Star and Long Run, and more positives than negatives come out of a defeat to only that pair, encouragingly matching his Wetherby form just 3 weeks on, not threatening but sticking to his task; he should remain competitive in Grade 1 staying chases, capable of winning slightly lesser ones than this. **Diamond Harry** had won first time in each previous season, but this reappearance came under different circumstances, injured after his impressive Hennessy win last year, and he shaped as if the run will bring him on, going comfortably until after 4 out but getting tired and spared a hard race once beaten; he could yet prove more competitive in other top staying chases. **Time For Rupert** was way off his best, looking laboured, and it probably came too soon for him after the Charlie Hall. **Pure Faith** was outclassed.

NEWBURY Saturday, Nov 26
GOOD

2777 Hennessy Gold Cup Chase (Hcap) (Gr 3) (1) (168) (4yo+) £85,425 — 3¼m110y (21)

Last run	Horse / Trainer / Age-Weight / Jockey	SP	Dist	Pos
2460^{3}	CARRUTHERS *MarkBradstock* 8-10-4^{146} (t) MattieBatchelor	12 10/1		1
3146^{5}	PLANET OF SOUND *PhilipHobbs* 9-11-2^{158} (t) RichardJohnson	11 14/1	3¾	2
2460^{6}	FAIR ALONG (GER) *PhilipHobbs* 9-10-0^{142} (s+t) MissNCarberry	33/1	¾	3
2461*	GREAT ENDEAVOUR (IRE) *DavidPipe* 7-10-9^{151} TimmyMurphy	5/1	½	4
4740*	Beshabar (IRE) *TimVaughan* 9-10-8^{150} AidanColeman	14 10/1	nk	5
4208^{pu}	Wymott (IRE) *DonaldMcCain* 7-10-2^{144} GrahamLee	10/1	1½	6
2461^{ur}	The Giant Bolster *DavidBridgwater* 6-10-4^{146} (s) TomScudamore	16/1	8	7
4740^{pu}	Blazing Bailey *AlanKing* 9-10-9^{151} RobertThornton	50/1	1½	8
2461^{f}	Tullamore Dew (IRE) *NickGifford* 9-10-0^{142} LiamTreadwell	25/1	½	9
	Michel Le Bon (FR) *PaulNicholls* 8-10-4^{146} NoelFehily	9 10/1	1½	10
2237^{2}	Aiteen Thirtythree (IRE) *PaulNicholls* 7-10-10^{152} RWalsh	5 9/2f	½	11
2460^{pu}	Balthazar King (IRE) *PhilipHobbs* 7-9-11^{142} GilesHawkins^{3}	66/1	20	12
2193	Muirhead (IRE) *NoelMeade,Ireland* 8-10-4^{146} PaulCarberry	20 18/1	10	13
2214^{2}	Qhilimar (FR) *CharlieLongsdon* 7-10-0^{142} (s) RichieMcGrath	33/1	28	14
2374*	Sarando *PaulWebber* 6-10-11^{153} (s+t) WillKennedy	22/1		f
4740^{6}	Neptune Collonges (FR) *PaulNicholls* 10-11-5^{168} HarryDerham^{7}	33/1		pu
4585^{4}	Wayward Prince *IanWilliams* 7-10-8^{150} DougieCostello	13/2 6/1		pu
2461^{5}	Billie Magern *NigelTwiston-Davies* 7-10-0^{142} SamTwiston-Davies	33/1		pu

3.10race The Oaksey Partnership 18ran 6m31.20

There was a lack of a stand-out second-season chaser in this year's Hennessy and none of those that fitted that bracket stepped up to the mark on the day, leaving some more established sorts to fill the places, so it can't be said to be a vintage renewal of what is one of the most prestigious handicaps in the calendar; it's typical of this track that positive tactics are favoured to some extent, especially in big-field chases with the fences coming thick and fast, and that seemed to be the case here despite a sound overall gallop, Carruthers making most and Planet of Sound never far away, either. **Carruthers** had become very well treated on his solid form in top graded races in 2009/10 and belatedly showed that he retains at least most of his ability, perhaps helped by the application of a tongue strap, as it was his finishing effort that was the difference from other recent efforts, still forcefully ridden and doing well to fend off various challenges from 4 out, particularly as he'd made a couple of mistakes in the early part of the race; the Welsh National is reportedly up next and, whilst others that have been targeted specifically at that race might stand more chance, Carruthers should remain with some handicapping scope on his best form. **Planet of Sound** had a couple of problems that meant he raced only twice last season (not at his best on either occasion), but he's clearly put those behind him as this was a cracking effort from a very high mark; so long as he stands more racing this time around, he should be competitive in graded races now, as he was in 2009/10 (Grade 1 winner that season). **Fair Along**'s jumping over fences leaves a lot to be desired nowadays and, as such, he's not a safe betting proposition, but to finish as close as he did despite blundering his way round (got behind early and almost unseated at the fourteenth) underlines that he is on a potentially lenient mark should everything click into place one day. **Great Endeavour**'s task in handicaps will be tougher from now on, under a 4 lb penalty this day for his Paddy Power win and due to be 6 lb higher still, but it's not out of the question that he improves some more this term, impressive at Cheltenham and, for much of this, shaping like the best horse at the weights; he made a big move between 4 out and 2 out to get from the back of the main group to be on terms with the leaders, an effort which took its toll to some extent, although the overriding impression is that he'll prove best up to 3m. **Beshabar**'s stamina is his main asset, as he showed in winning the Scottish National when last seen in April, and it bodes well for a return to marathon trips that he ran to form despite not seeming sufficiently tested, outpaced approaching the straight and coming back strongly towards the finish; he could develop into a leading Grand National contender this season, but the Welsh National next month makes even more appeal for him. **Wymott** strikes as having the ability to be competitive from his mark, with some of his novice form reading well, but suspicions are beginning to creep in over his attitude, unwilling when tried in cheekpieces in last season's RSA, and, even with them discarded on this first start since, failing to convince that he was putting everything in, carrying his head rather high and also hanging left between 3 out and 2 out. **The Giant Bolster** isn't the safest jumper and showed reluctance at the start this day, but all things considered he shaped better than the result, travelling smoothly enough into the straight despite not having been that fluent, whilst he was quite badly hampered by Sarando's fall at the sixteenth, too. **Blazing Bailey** is high enough in the weights again after 2 wins last term and, although not totally discredited on this return, he did have one of his rather lazy days and was never fully competitive. **Tullamore Dew** had never been tried beyond 21f previously and left the impression he was stretched by the trip, going as well as any until after 5 out but not picking up; there has been enough in both the Paddy Power and this to suggest his mark isn't a problem. **Michel Le Bon** has had injury problems that kept him off the track since an impressive chasing debut in a Grade 2 novice at this meeting in 2009 and probably just found this too tough an ask for his belated return, prominent until 4 out and not unduly knocked about once held; it remains to be seen whether he retains all of his ability, but he's in excellent hands and could yet come good. **Aiteen Thirtythree** ran better than the result suggests, holding every chance 4 out and still challenging for a place at the second last, not unduly punished once held; it might just be that he's not that well treated, though. **Balthazar King**'s jumping has gone to pot with an attacking policy not having been adopted on his last 3 starts, a smaller field perhaps ideal for him. **Muirhead** was going okay until blundering at the fifteenth and then was slightly hampered at the next, not persevered with in the end. **Qhilimar** has been reluctant in the past and didn't appear to take much interest here, his being 5 lb out of the weights not the issue. **Sarando** is on a stiff mark but was still close up when crashing out at the sixteenth. **Neptune Collonges** isn't as good or reliable as he once was, his best effort last term hardly the most solid form, and he never threatened to get involved on this return. **Wayward Prince** blundered at the eighth and was immediately struggling; he was a smart novice chaser last term and could yet do better, though he will have to cut out the mistakes to make an impact in top handicaps. **Billie Magern** again found it all too much; he should stay this far.

KEMPTON Monday, Dec 26
GOOD

3283 William Hill King George VI Chase (Gr 1) (1) (4yo+) £102,992 — 3m (18)

2621*	KAUTO STAR (FR) *PaulNicholls* 11-11-10 (t) RWalsh	11/4 3/1		1
2621[2]	LONG RUN (FR) *NickyHenderson* 6-11-10 MrSWaley-Cohen	11/10 1/1f	1¼	2
2256[ur]	CAPTAIN CHRIS (IRE) *PhilipHobbs* 7-11-10 (t) RichardJohnson	8/1	17	3
3001[2]	Somersby (IRE) *HenriettaKnight* 7-11-10 (t) DominicElsworth	14 12/1	½	4
2907[3]	Nacarat (FR) *TomGeorge* 10-11-10 (t) PaddyBrennan	40/1	22	5
2899*	Golan Way *SheenaWest* 7-11-10 MarcGoldstein	66/1		ref
2612*	Master Minded (FR) *PaulNicholls* 8-11-10 DarylJacob	11/2		pu

3.10race Mr Clive D. Smith 7ran 6m02.00

For as long as people race horses over fences, this race will be spoken of with awe, as great a match as has occured in this championship race's history, 2 outstanding chasers at the top of their game leaving some high-class opposition for dead in the closing stages, the winner simply superb in gaining an unprecedented fifth win in this, testament to his ability, durability and jumping prowess, his performance as good as any in this race, bar his own fourth win, since the days of Desert Orchid, the runner-up good enough to have won the majority of runnings in the last 20 years; the pace was sound, the tempo much more even than for the earlier Feltham for novices. **Kauto Star** gained a scarcely believable fifth win in this event, a performance in its way every bit as perfect as his fourth victory 2 years previously, up against a top-notch opponent this time yet not allowing that one a full chance thanks in part to a more positive ride than he received, jumping faultlessly, always travelling with great economy and, having led at the eighth, soon stretching the field after the twelfth, around 4 lengths up after 4 out and maintaining the gallop over the last 3 fences; it was perhaps significant that, as well as looking in superb shape, that his demeanour beforehand was in marked contrast to before this race and the Gold Cup last season, seeming much more relaxed; he is now likely to bid for a third Gold Cup, and another stunning battle ought to be in store between he and Long Run, the duo a class apart from the rest, though the feeling remains that the stiffer stamina test and likely stronger pace in the Gold Cup will suit Long Run more than him; a mention also for Paul Nicholls, whose exploits in getting Kauto Star back to such a high level clearly reflects extremely well, this win potentially the one that allows the trainer to again fend off Nicky Henderson in the title race. **Long Run** confirmed the positive impression created at Haydock and lost nothing in defeat against one of the outstanding chasers, beaten fair and square but still with every chance of gaining a second win in the Gold Cup, his form and that of the winner head and shoulders above that of any of their likely rivals at the moment, tactics plus less fluent (but not poor) jumping making a difference to this outcome, closing strongly come the end after Kauto Star had essentially sealed the race when pressing on after the twelfth, the longer trip at Cheltenham more in his favour than the winner's; he didn't run between the King George and Gold Cup last season, though the former was 3 weeks later and he wasn't on the back of 2 defeats, so it might be he'll take in the renamed Betfair Denman Chase at Newbury prior to a potentially superiority deciding clash between the pair (score currently 2-2) in March. **Captain Chris**, taking a big step up in trip, possibly hadn't had the ideal prep after his mishap at Exeter, missing at least one intended engagement, but he essentially looked short of the class required at this level, hard at work in rear after the winner pressed on, closing under pressure to chase the first 2 into the straight but readily left behind over the last 3 fences, far from disgraced all the same, especially considering he'd been short of room entering the straight; the Ryanair may be the race for him at Cheltenham. **Somersby**, who looked to have come on since Huntingdon and who was tongue tied first time, ended up running creditably on paper, although he remains something of an enigma, not shaping as if nearly so well suited by the trip as might have been expected, looking a danger to all 4 out but once again failing to quicken when it mattered in a top race and unable to get past the labouring Captain Chris for third; he'll have something to prove when next seen, although with Master Minded on the sidelines, the Ascot Chase in February becomes a more winnable target. **Nacarat** has a good record here, including twice running with credit in this race, but he just doesn't seem quite the force he was and dropped away from 6 out, running no better than he had previously this autumn. **Golan Way** just couldn't cope with this level of competition and had long since dropped out of contention having blundered at the eighth when he refused 4 out, out on his feet and best given the benefit of the doubt again so far as his attitude is concerned. **Master Minded** wasn't sure to stay 3m but he was beaten before lack of stamina became an issue, a rare mistake, at the thirteenth, seeming to unsettle him, well held when pulled up before the last, reportedly suffering a serious injury, one which may end his career, which would be a downbeat end on the track for one of the great chasers of recent times.

LEOPARDSTOWN Wednesday, Dec 28 GOOD to SOFT

3382 Lexus Chase (Gr 1) (5yo+) £77,500 — 3m (17)

2620[3]	SYNCHRONISED (IRE) *JonjoO'Neill,GB* 8-11-10 APMcCoy	8/1		1
3076*	RUBI LIGHT (FR) *RobertHennessy* 6-11-10 AELynch	9/4	8½	2
2340*	QUITO DE LA ROQUE (FR) *ColmAMurphy* 7-11-10 DavyRussell	13/8f	2½	3
3043	Roberto Goldback (IRE) *DTHughes* 9-11-10 MissNCarberry	25/1	2¾	4
*3696**	Noland *PaulNicholls,GB* 10-11-10 (t) RWalsh	10/1	3¾	5
235*	Follow The Plan (IRE) *OliverMcKiernan* 8-11-10 TJDoyle	33/1	27	6
3076[2]	Joncol (IRE) *PaulNolan* 8-11-10 BarryGeraghty	11/2	4¼	7
4208[4]	Magnanimity (IRE) *DTHughes* 7-11-10 BryanJCooper	20/1	¾	8
3076[3]	Cooldine (IRE) *WPMullins* 9-11-10 DJCasey	20/1	26	9

2.35race Mr John P. McManus 9ran 6m17.40

A Lexus which did much to highlight the ongoing dearth of talent among staying chasers in Ireland, and it went for export for the fifth time in the last 6 years; the pace was steady and the time was slower than the Fort Leney for novices earlier on the card. **Synchronised** sidestepped a bid for a repeat Welsh National win in favour of a belated first crack at graded level over fences and the move paid off in spades as he proved far too strong for the best Ireland has to offer over this trip, not always foot perfect tracking the leaders, pushed along in fourth after 3 out and staying on strongly to take command before the last, leaving the inside only briefly there then ridden clear; he's well worth his place in the Gold Cup after this, as likely as any to pick up the pieces if either Kauto Star or Long Run underperform. **Rubi Light** opened up more options in staying this longer trip but it'll surely be only on Irish soil that he picks up any further races at this level, the Hennessy here the obvious one for him to go for next; things panned out well for him, racing close to a steady pace before going on at the tenth, but he never looked like getting away and was overwhelmed by the winner on the run to the last. **Quito de La Roque** had his Gold Cup hopes blown to pieces yet there's little reason to suspect he won't continue to prove a force in the top staying races in Ireland, travelling and jumping with greater fluency than usual until slightly slow 2 out but unable to turn it on in the latter stages in the way he has against lesser opposition, actually losing ground on the runner-up after edging right on the approach to the last. **Roberto Goldback** showed he's as good as he was for Jessica Harrington and turned the form around with the pair in front of him at Thurles in November, dropping to the rear briefly before 5 out but soon back in contention and sticking to his task. **Noland** is unlikely to recapture the form which saw him land the John Durkan in 2008, this just his fourth start since, but it was a pleasing first run since his win in the AON Chase at Newbury in February, leading or disputing the lead until the tenth, making his only semblance of an error 4 out and still in contention for a place early in the straight. **Follow The Plan** shaped as if in need of this first start since his unlikely Grade 1 win in May, not always fluent held up, making headway on the outer in the back straight and gradually losing touch with the principals from 3 out. **Joncol** is beginning to look like he needs headgear and never looked like making it 3 places in this race in succession, niggled along before a mistake at the ninth and running on far too late having been adrift of the principals by 3 out. **Magnanimity** is possibly going to be brought along for a crack at the National knowing his trainer and clearly needed this, beaten much further than looked likely on the home turn, but he surely needs more experience before he can be considered a contender for Aintree, making a few minor errors here. **Cooldine** has an appalling record in this race and mistakes 5 out and 4 out were enough to put paid to his chance this time.

CHELTENHAM Tuesday, Mar 13 GOOD (Old Course)

4592 William Hill Supreme Nov Hdle (Gr 1) (1) (4yo+) £56,950 — 2m110y (8)

Last run	Horse, trainer, age-weight, jockey		SP	Dist
3797 *	CINDERS AND ASHES *DonaldMcCain* 5-11-7 JasonMaguire	11	10/1	
4118 f	DARLAN *NickyHenderson* 5-11-7 APMcCoy	6	7/1	1¼
4004 *	TRIFOLIUM (FR) *CharlesByrnes,Ireland* 5-11-7 (s) DavyRussell	11	15/2	nk
4119 *	Montbazon (FR) *AlanKing* 5-11-7 RobertThornton	8	15/2	hd
3595 4	Prospect Wells (FR) *PaulNicholls* 7-11-7 (t) RWalsh	16	14/1	½
4003 *	Allure of Illusion (IRE) *WPMullins,Ireland* 6-11-7 (t) DavyCondon		40/1	8
4084 *	Galileo's Choice (IRE) *DKWeld,Ireland* 6-11-7 MrRobbieMcNamara	7	6/1f	sh
3813 3	Distant Memories (IRE) *TomJTaaffe,Ireland* 6-11-7 AELynch		33/1	1¾
4025 *	Tetlami (IRE) *NickyHenderson* 6-11-7 BarryGeraghty	11	12/1	sh
4119 2	Vulcanite (IRE) *CharlieLongsdon* 5-11-7 PaddyBrennan		22/1	2¼
3475	Jimbill (IRE) *TimVaughan* 6-11-7 AidanColeman		100/1	½
4277 *	Agent Archie (USA) *DonaldMcCain* 5-11-7 HenryBrooke		50/1	1¾
4119 f	Colour Squadron (IRE) *PhilipHobbs* 6-11-7 RichardJohnson		14/1	hd
2449 *	Steps To Freedom (IRE) *MrsJHarrington,Ireland* 6-11-7 (t) RobbiePower	7	13/2	5
3813 *	Midnight Game *WPMullins,Ireland* 5-11-7 PaulTownend		18/1	sh
3813 2	Dylan Ross (IRE) *NoelMeade,Ireland* 6-11-7 (b) PaulCarberry		20/1	1
4135 4	Hazy Tom (IRE) *CharlieLongsdon* 6-11-7 NoelFehily		33/1	5
3909	Catch Tammy (IRE) *DavidPipe* 6-11-7 TomScudamore		200/1	4
4004 2	Simenon (IRE) *WPMullins,Ireland* 5-11-7 DJCasey		50/1	1

1.30race Dermot Hanafin & Phil Cunningham 19ran 3m52.20

It hasn't looked a vintage season in the 2-mile novice division, with nothing having shown form above the usual standard for a Supreme winner, and that 5 of them finished bunched up means there is still no clear-cut standard set; the tight finish was in part due to a gallop that was no more than fair—they went quite a bit slower than in the Champion Hurdle—and those that were ridden close up certainly weren't at a disadvantage, with the race not really taking shape until between 3 out and 2 out. **Cinders And Ashes** was one of just a handful that took the eye in the preliminaries, looking in fine shape, and he showed what he's truly about after 3 easy wins on heavy ground in the North, confirming the positive impression created in each of them, and, whilst this somewhat muddling affair isn't conclusive evidence that he's the top 2m novice of the season, there's no doubt he's amongst the best of them and remains open to progress; a good position helped him the way the race went, never too far away and hugging the inner throughout, but he did well to recover quickly from a blunder at the fourth and showed a likeable response to pressure to lead before the last, flattening that flight as well but still staying on strongly. **Darlan** is taken to prove just about the best of these in time, the highest rated coming into this after shaping so well in handicap company last month, and under different circumstances he might well have won this, starting his effort from further back than ideal and also forced wide with his effort, staying on strongly but too late after not being totally fluent at the last; a longer trip won't be a problem—he may even benefit from it—and the 2½m novice at Aintree next month could be an ideal race if it doesn't come too soon. **Trifolium** proved himself on a much bigger stage after some small-field wins in Ireland and could progress again from here, his strong-travelling style promising more for sure, going as well as any into the straight, and there's a chance that he'd have found more but for a minor slip on the final bend; 2m will always be his trip. **Montbazon** is another with ongoing potential, in his case not just as a hurdler, as he has the size for chasing, but he'll need to learn to jump more fluently if he's to go as high as he could, leading between the last 2 flights but not helped by further slight errors at both. **Prospect Wells** hadn't been himself in the Tolworth in early-January but, following a breathing operation and fitted with a tongue tie, he bounced back with his best effort yet over hurdles, rather surprisingly getting outpaced when the tempo increased and closing up well again at the finish. **Allure of Illusion** improved in face of a stiff task on only his third start over hurdles, no threat but plugging on from towards the back, matching the useful form he showed in bumpers last season; as one so lightly raced with Willie Mullins, there could be even more to come, though probably only over hurdles judged on his looks and pedigree. **Galileo's Choice** wasn't seen to best effect, patiently ridden and taken to the outer to begin his effort approaching the second last, not knocked about when it was clear he wasn't going to get there; there's plenty of time yet for him to do better as a hurdler, though his jumping needs some work on this evidence. **Distant Memories** is inexperienced in this sphere and remains likely to prove capable of better, smart on the Flat and not seen to best effect here, taking a keen hold in last position and not unduly knocked about. **Tetlami** came unstuck up in grade, simply not seeming good enough after turning into the straight with every chance; top-end handicaps are likely to be his level next season. **Vulcanite** still has things to learn as a hurdler, not fluent on occasions here, whilst he could do with settling down a bit, but there's something in the locker if/when everything comes together, as indicated by his lasting on the bridle until 2 out here; he could be the type to do well in good-quality handicaps next season. **Jimbill** wasn't up to the task, well positioned but soon beaten once things developed after 3 out. **Agent Archie**'s potential is for a lower level than this, the task simply proving beyond him after cutting out a lot of the running. **Colour Squadron** is better than he showed here, his form that ties in with Montbazon proving as much, and it may be that he was still feeling the effects of his fall less than a month ago. **Steps To Freedom** faced his first big test as a hurdler and disappointed, always in rear and beaten after a slight mistake 3 out; he was reported afterwards to be coughing. **Midnight Game** is an edgy sort and this occasion seemed too much for him, sweating up beforehand and proving far too keen in the race. **Dylan Ross** met trouble up the inside, but it was his jumping that seemed the main issue in this big field. **Hazy Tom**'s season has been underwhelming after such a promising start, but long term he's not one to be giving up on, very much a chaser on looks, this effort itself too bad to be true. **Catch Tammy** had no chance at this level and lost touch immediately when the race began to take shape. **Simenon** unsurprisingly found the task beyond him; he's not much on looks.

4593 Racing Post Arkle Challenge Trophy Chase (Gr 1) (1) (5yo+) £74,035 2m (13)

4116[*] SPRINTER SACRE (FR) *NickyHenderson* 6-11-7 BarryGeraghty 4/5 8/11f
3437[*] CUE CARD *ColinTizzard* 6-11-7 JoeTizzard 7 13/2 7
3913[f] MENORAH (IRE) *PhilipHobbs* 7-11-7 RichardJohnson 9 10/1 22
3794[3] Al Ferof (FR) *PaulNicholls* 7-11-7 RWalsh 7/2 3/1 3¼
3941[5] Blackstairmountain (IRE) *WPMullins,Ireland* 7-11-7 (t) PaulTownend 20/1 3¼
4178[2] Foildubh (IRE) *JohnPatrickRyan,Ireland* 8-11-7 RobertColgan 66/1 37
2.05race Mrs Caroline Mould 6ran 3m48.30

A particularly small field for the championship event for 2m novice chasers, the quality of the favourite a large part of that, Peddlers Cross and Flemenstar notable among the absentees, though whether that pair, good as they are, could have made any impression on an outstanding winner is doubtful; the pace seemed no more than fair early on, though half the field were struggling to keep up after halfway. **Sprinter Sacre** had scared away most of the opposition with the ease of his earlier wins over fences and routed those that did turn up with a performance that marks him out as an outstanding prospect, the best winner of this race since Azertyuiop and with the potential to go as far as that great 2m chaser did, already a short-priced favourite for the 2013 Champion Chase; he wasn't extended, cruising behind the leaders until left in front at the tenth, soon going clear and, though closed on in the straight, quickening impressively when asked after the last and sauntering clear, having plenty more to give at the line. **Cue Card** has done very well over fences, unfortunate not to be unbeaten on completed starts coming into this, and while he was no match for the winner here he emerged with plenty of credit and could well be a leading candidate for the Ryanair in a year's time, his jumping generally pretty solid; he led to the ninth and rallied before 2 out, though any hopes that he might challenge a vulnerable leader were soon snuffed out as that rival sauntered away. **Menorah**'s jumping just didn't hold up in the latter stages, disputing second when not fluent 3 out, hitting the next and slow into the last, though he'd been at work for some time to reach the position he did 3 out and left the impression he wasn't at his best on the day; a season which had promised much has fallen apart and his future in this sphere depends heavily on his jumping shortcomings being sorted out. **Al Ferof**, on his toes, lost his chance by taking off much too soon and banking the tenth, in a narrow lead at the time; his earlier form shows he clearly has the ability to win more races, though which ones may well depend on avoiding Sprinter Sacre. **Blackstairmountain** just isn't good enough to compete at this level and, having been held up, could make no impression when shaken up after 4 out; he's a smart performer and will be placed to win races again in Ireland, but he's likely to continue to be found wanting when taking on opponents of this quality. **Foildubh** was outclassed, more patiently ridden than usual and struggling to keep in touch from before halfway, the less testing ground than he usually races on merely incidental.

4595 **Stan James Champion Hdle Challenge Trophy (Gr 1) (1) (4yo+)** £210,715 — 2m110y (8)

3282 2	ROCK ON RUBY (IRE) *PaulNicholls* 7-11-10 (t) NoelFehily 10	11/1		1
3282 3	OVERTURN (IRE) *DonaldMcCain* 8-11-10 JasonMaguire	20/1	3¾	2
3943 *	HURRICANE FLY (IRE) *WPMullins,Ireland* 8-11-10 RWalsh 8/11	4/6f	1¾	3
4149 *	Binocular (FR) *NickyHenderson* 8-11-10 APMcCoy 5	4/1	1	4
4118 *	Zarkandar (IRE) *PaulNicholls* 5-11-10 DarylJacob 8	9/1	hd	5
3943 2	Oscars Well (IRE) *MrsJHarrington,Ireland* 7-11-10 RobbiePower	14/1	1¼	6
4118	Brampour (IRE) *PaulNicholls* 5-11-10 HarryDerham	50/1	3½	7
4155 *	Zaidpour (FR) *WPMullins,Ireland* 6-11-10 PaulTownend	22/1	½	8
4149 2	Celestial Halo (IRE) *PaulNicholls* 8-11-10 (b+t) HarrySkelton	50/1	5	9
4155 2	Kalann (IRE) *SabrinaJHarty,Ireland* 5-11-10 MichaelDarcy	150/1	16	10

3.20race The Festival Goers 10ran 3m48.90

An outstanding Champion Hurdle winner in Hurricane Fly couldn't repeat his victory of 12 months earlier but this was still an above-average running, the winner's performance the best in the race, apart from Hurricane Fly's, in the last decade; there were significant absentees, Oscar Whisky and Grandouet the most notable, and that pair along with Spirit Son, who has missed the whole season, may well enter consideration in 2013; the feature here was the pace, the runner-up ridden to ensure a true gallop all the way, and though the first 2 were well positioned all the way, sectionals suggest their advantage may only have been marginal over those held up in rear. **Rock On Ruby**, apart from Zarkandar, the least exposed in the field, showed himself a top-class hurdler, building on his efforts earlier in the season which promised much, the run of the race and his position in it perfect for showing him to best advantage, comfortable racing just behind a good pace and, jumping fluently, having the turn of foot required to go on after 2 out, still not with the matter settled at the last but finding plenty and drawing away at the finish; whether he'd be quite so effective behind a steadier pace is open to question, and the make-up of the field and likely tempo are likely to be serious considerations when weighing up his chance in this race another year, though in form terms he will surely be close to the best in the field. **Overturn** is a most admirable racehorse, extremely tough, game and genuine, and he turned in another splendid performance, freshened up after Kempton was a race too many before the turn of the year, a runner in his own right in contrast to last year and ridden to ensure a thorough test at the trip, forcing the pace and, though having to give best to the winner after 2 out, sticking most resolutely to his task to fend off the challenge of the third at the last; given his age, his demanding races are likely to catch up with him at some point, though hopefully not for a while yet, his effort here and overall record reflecting tremendous credit on his trainer in keeping him sweet. **Hurricane Fly**, who was sweating a touch but essentially looked okay for him, wasn't at his best; held up in rear, he made headway 3 out but hadn't reached the leaders by the time he came under pressure at the next, and although he was closing at the last his effort told; there's every chance he'll bounce back at Punchestown, though his limited campaign this season and previous fragility make him an unappealing ante-post prospect for regaining his crown next March. **Binocular** made the frame in this for a third time, having missed last year's renewal in controversial circumstances, though not quite at his best on this occasion, and while in hindsight he might have done better with a more forward ride, asked instead to track Hurricane Fly at the back of the field, he took too long to hit full stride after that rival made his move, staying on strongly going to the last only for a mistake there to stall his momentum again; he might again make an impact in some of the trial races in the build-up to next year's Champion, but he seems unlikely ever to regain his crown. **Zarkandar**, who didn't take the eye beforehand and was on his toes, lost his unbeaten record over hurdles, facing by far his stiffest task, emerging with credit for his finishing effort after being tapped for foot down the hill; he requires a step up in trip at this level, and ought to be more at ease in the Aintree Hurdle over 2½m next month. **Oscars Well** ran respectably, though he was ridden closer to the pace than the trio that finished immediately in front of him and as such may have had a slight advantage; unlike most in this field, he is likely to make at least as good a chaser as hurdler and could well return a leading contender for the Arkle or Golden Miller in a year's time. **Brampour**, whose rider was unable to claim, ran about as well as he's able, though his was a rather flat effort; he's shown himself a high-class hurdler at 2m this season but lacks scope and has reached his level, any prospect of improvement to come in future lying with a step up in trip. **Zaidpour** needed to improve to compete at this level and wasn't able to, though he ran better than the distance beaten indicates, in sixth, around 3 lengths behind Binocular, when he made a bad mistake at the last; he's evidently versatile with regard to distance and will continue to thrive closer to home, given the opportunities for a horse of his ability in the Irish programme. **Celestial Halo**, in the frame in 2 previous attempts in this race, has had an excellent season but this was a far more searching test of his ability and he was found wanting, trying to mix it with the first 2 but giving way 3 out and soon out of contention; he has a mixed record at Aintree, that his last outing of the season in all 4 previous campaigns. **Kalann**, on his toes, was a highly optimistic participant and didn't get a look-in in a truly-run race, always in the last pair.

4597 OLBG Mares' Hdle (David Nicholson) (Gr 2) (1) (4yo+ f+m) £39,389 — 2½m (9)

Ref	Horse, trainer, age-weight, jockey	SP	Dist	Pos
262*	QUEVEGA (FR) *WPMullins,Ireland* 8-11-5 RWalsh	8/13 4/7f		1
3792[2]	KENTFORD GREY LADY *EmmaLavelle* 6-11-0 NoelFehily	14/1	4	2
3771[4]	GOLDEN SUNBIRD (IRE) *PaulNolan,Ireland* 8-11-3 (t) RobbiePower	66/1	nk	3
3912*	Alasi *PaulWebber* 8-11-5 DominicElsworth	20/1	nk	4
3069[2]	Shop Dj (IRE) *PeterFahey,Ireland* 7-11-5 (t) DavyRussell	10/1	nk	5
4331[3]	Cloudy Spirit *RegHollinshead* 7-11-0 TimmyMurphy	33/1	½	6
1991*	Ixora (IRE) *JamieSnowden* 6-11-0 TomO'Brien	50/1	¾	7
3592*	Kells Belle (IRE) *NickyHenderson* 6-11-5 BarryGeraghty	33/1	hd	8
4134[3]	Swincombe Flame *NickWilliams* 6-11-0 WillKennedy	12 10/1	sh	9
3792[3]	Our Girl Salley (IRE) *MrsPrunellaDobbs,Ireland* 7-11-5 AELynch	20/1	½	10
3929	What A Charm (IRE) *ALTMoore,Ireland* 5-11-3 (b) PaulCarberry	40/1	½	11
4169[4]	Dorabelle (IRE) *DonaldMcCain* 7-11-0 JasonMaguire	100/1	2¾	12
3847[2]	Tempest River (IRE) *BenCase* 6-11-0 AidanColeman	100/1	1	13
4365*	Dare To Doubt *WPMullins,Ireland* 8-11-5 PaulTownend	40/1	1¼	14
3792*	Violin Davis (FR) *PaulNicholls* 6-11-5 (t) DarylJacob	28/1	2	15
4025	The Strawberry One *DavidArbuthnot* 7-11-0 DenisO'Regan	100/1	14	16
4269[f]	Terre du Vent (FR) *TomGeorge* 6-11-0 PaddyBrennan	20/1	3	17
2876[3]	Candelita *JoHughes* 5-11-0 MarkGrant	150/1	¾	18
4436[6]	Himayna *FrankSheridan* 8-11-0 GilesHawkins	200/1	64	19

4.40race Hammer & Trowel Syndicate 19ran 4m51.00

A slow gallop made for a messy renewal, things developing into a sprint after 2 out, the heaped finish for the places holding down the bare form; it made no difference to Quevega, though, who won this race easily for the fourth consecutive year. **Quevega** tends to find this her easiest task of the season and has won each of the last 4 renewals with loads in hand, the lack of pace on here making no difference to her, cruising along in mid-field and accelerating to the front in familiar fashion on the run to the last; the Grade 1 over 3m at Punchestown that she's won for the past 2 seasons looks sure to be her target again and, with this suggesting she's as good as ever, she'll clearly hold strong claims again. **Kentford Grey Lady** added further to the good impression that she's made previously this season, and the feeling is that the best of her is still to come, doing well as best of the rest behind Quevega here, especially as the slow pace at this trip wouldn't have suited; good-quality handicaps remain an option, whilst some of the other top mares races should also be within her capabilities. **Golden Sunbird** got back on track over hurdles again after almost 2 months off, returning to the sort of form she was showing at around this time last season, with every chance from a prominent position; she's not the biggest, so it's perhaps no surprise that she hasn't proved as good over fences. **Alasi** gave her running as usual, and in typical style, moving up from the back going strongly and, but for slight interference approaching 3 out, likely to have been challenging for second. **Shop Dj**'s wide-margin win at Punchestown last year showed that she's an above-average mare, and she shaped as well as any behind Quevega here, unsuited by patient tactics in a steadily-run race and finishing strongly. **Cloudy Spirit** rarely fails to give her running and was close to her best here despite getting caught in some trouble on the bend before 3 out; she also races mostly at 3m, so this relative test of speed probably wasn't ideal. **Ixora** progressed in the summer/autumn and finishing quite close up in this Grade 2 contest underlines how far she's come this season, albeit without ever being too far away from the steady pace; she seems to handle firmish ground particularly well and will presumably be kept on the go now. **Kells Belle** was up further in class and not quite up to it despite showing her form, leading briefly before Quevega but soon put in her place, run out of the places on the flat. **Swincombe Flame** is still one to have on the radar, the steady pace here working against her as much as any, and there's no doubting that her recent handicap form is strong; she also has the size to take well to fences when the time comes. **Our Girl Salley** is consistent in the main and a wide position didn't help her cause here, weakening on the run-in having made progress from the back. **What A Charm** seemed to run as well as ever in form terms, but this was a messy race and she looked a hard ride, racing in snatches and merely plugging on; she was wearing blinkers instead of cheekpieces, incidentally. **Dorabelle** wasn't discredited faced with a stiff task, though after dictating the pace she was easily brushed aside. **Tempest River** had no chance at this level and made no impression. **Dare To Doubt** struggled back over hurdles in this higher grade, beaten quickly when the sprint began; her impressive handicap win in November remains a standout effort. **Violin Davis** wasn't on her game for some reason, beaten as soon as the race started to take shape; her overall record suggests she'll soon bounce back. **The Strawberry One**'s yard have had a quiet time of things for most of the season and, other than her fifth in a handicap at Kempton in December, she's been out of sorts since the summer. **Terre du Vent** will have to improve her jumping if she's to achieve all that she might, a blunder at the fifth most notable here, but she was also messed around going to 3 out and spared a hard race after; she'll still win races over hurdles. **Candelita** was way out of her depth.

CHELTENHAM Wednesday, Mar 14
GOOD (Old Course)

4607 Neptune Investment Management Nov Hdle (Baring Bingham) (Gr 1) (1) (4yo+) £56,950 — 2m5f (10)

4072*	SIMONSIG *NickyHenderson* 6-11-7 BarryGeraghty	9/4 2/1f		
4304*	FELIX YONGER (IRE) *WPMullins,Ireland* 6-11-7 PaulTownend	16/1	7	
3620*	MONKSLAND (IRE) *NoelMeade,Ireland* 5-11-7 PaulCarberry	9/2 11/2	11	
3121*	Close House *DavidPipe* 5-11-7 TomScudamore	33/1	4½	
4054[2]	Sous Les Cieux (FR) *WPMullins,Ireland* 6-11-7 (t) RWalsh	11/2	1¾	
4226[2]	Nagpur (FR) *VenetiaWilliams* 6-11-7 AidanColeman	66/1	9	
3944[3]	Make Your Mark (IRE) *WPMullins,Ireland* 5-11-7 DavyRussell	8 15/2	¾	
4118	Double Ross (IRE) *NigelTwiston-Davies* 6-11-7 SamTwiston-Davies	33/1	3	
4167*	Fiulin *DavidPipe* 7-11-7 (b) ConorO'Farrell	80/1	2¾	
4054*	Beneficient (IRE) *AJMartin,Ireland* 6-11-7 BryanJCooper	16 14/1	8	
3762*	Nelson's Bridge (IRE) *NickyHenderson* 5-11-7 APMcCoy	18 16/1	5	
3909[3]	Secret Edge *AlanKing* 4-10-12 WayneHutchinson	25/1	2	
4295*	Sunny Ledgend *AndrewMartin* 7-11-7 MrSDrinkwater	100/1	¾	
1262*	Natural High (IRE) *PaulRich* 7-11-7 TomDoyle	100/1	77	
4167[2]	Brass Tax (IRE) *BenCase* 6-11-7 DarylJacob	100/1	6	
3698*	Cotton Mill *JohnFerguson* 5-11-7 DenisO'Regan	8/1		u
4518[3]	Baldadash (IRE) *GeorgeBaker* 7-11-7 PaulMoloney	200/1		pu

2.05race Mr R. A. Bartlett 17ran 4m57.40

A top renewal of the Baring Bingham and it looks sure to prove informative for open races at the top level next season, Simonsig a most impressive winner, and he's not the only one in the field with further potential; Fiulin raced in a clear lead for a long way, though the main pack essentially ignored him, going a fair pace themselves, with things developing fully once Cotton Mill took over after 4 out—the main incident of the race came when he veered left and unseated 2 out, hampering Monksland in particular. **Simonsig** is an outstanding novice, likely to end the season as the highest rated in this division (at any trip) in 2011/12, and he looks certain to go on and make his mark at the very highest level in open races if kept over hurdles next season, that appealing as the best option for one who has made such a huge impression in a handful of starts in this sphere, especially as he continues to give the impression that he'll prove equally effective around 2m, potentially a serious Champion Hurdle contender next year, acknowledging that his trainer has a few options already in that division; he really couldn't have been more impressive here, achieving a level of form above the average Neptune winner—no mean feat in itself given it's been won by such as Peddlers Cross in recent years—and he's value for a bigger winning margin, too, cruising up to Cotton Mill when that one ran out at the second last and extending his lead over the rest without coming off the bridle; given his physique and background in points, there is no doubt that Simonsig will also be a very exciting prospect for novice chasing should connections opt to go down that route with him next season. **Felix Yonger** turned in an excellent effort and wouldn't have been far off winning this in an average year, no match only for one who looks right out of the top drawer, and he could progress even more given how far he's come in just 4 starts over hurdles; waited with, he made smooth progress between 3 out and 2 out to challenge for the places, never on terms with Simonsig but pulling clear of the rest after left in second 2 out. **Monksland** would have finished closer to Felix Yonger but for getting hampered when Cotton Mill ran out at the second last, squeezing up the inner with his effort at that point, but it's unlikely that he'd have improved on the form of his defeat of Lyreen Legend in Ireland the time before, and it may be that he's reached his limit for the time being; his looks are a positive going forward, and he should be the sort to make a chaser. **Close House** duly upped his game faced with a much stiffer task, showing useful form, and there could be better still to come given that he seems not to have fully got to grips with hurdling yet (hit the fourth hard here), plus he's unexposed for a test of stamina, the way he saw this out not only suggesting that the longer trip suited, but that he'll probably stay even further. **Sous Les Cieux** has already proved that he's capable of better form than he showed here, even if his Royal Bond win has taken some knocks, and this was an odd performance, seemingly travelling okay at the third last but still with an awful lot of ground to make up and almost looking set to be eased off, but he began to stay on in the straight and was nearest at the finish, the trip appearing to be no problem. **Nagpur** was never likely to be good enough for a top novice like this, though perhaps the less testing ground than he'd faced before didn't suit, either, given that he raced lazily and merely plugged on past tired horses in the straight. **Make Your Mark** seemed likely to make a bigger impact for much of the race, challenging for third entering the straight, but it was disconcerting that he found so little up the hill; he's a point winner, but his size hardly suggests that he'll make a better chaser. **Double Ross** has proved himself a fairly useful novice but no better, and this level of competition was beyond him; he is bred to make a chaser and stay longer trips, and that's probably the way to go next season. **Fiulin** took a big step up in class after winning a very ordinay novice on his first start for this yard and, having been allowed to race clear, he was reeled in by the pack and struggling before 3 out. **Benefficient**'s Grade 1 win from Sous Les Cieux doesn't look a particularly strong piece of form, nor the most solid, but he shaped here as if there might have been some kind of problem, weakenking quickly from 2 out and tending to hang. **Nelson's Bridge** was aimed too high too soon in all likelihood and didn't jump well enough, though once held he wasn't knocked about, and the experience won't have been lost on him; his long-term future probably lies over fences, well made and bred for chasing. **Secret Edge** never travelled after hitting the sixth; up to this point he's been consistent over hurdles, so he should soon bounce back. **Sunny Ledgend** has done well in lesser novices and simply found this level beyond him. **Natural High** had little chance in this grade and was tailed off throughout; it was a weakish race that he won on his hurdling debut for Dermot Weld and he'd been bought of that yard since well held on the Flat in September. **Brass Tax** has it in him to win an ordinary novice but was punching well above his weight here. **Cotton Mill**'s Warwick win looks better after Ambion Wood's subsequent handicap success and he was set to show improvement himself before veering left and unseating when still in front approaching the second last, still going well enough at the time, but he is a fairly speedy horse for this trip over hurdles and the suspicion is that the first 2 would both have passed him; this was hopefully just a one-off incident and he's not one to have reservations about in terms of temperament. **Baldadash** was totally out of his depth.

4608 RSA Chase (Gr 1) (1) (5yo+) £74,035 3m110y (19)

4131[2]	BOBS WORTH (IRE) *NickyHenderson* 7-11-4 BarryGeraghty	9/2		1
3380[2]	FIRST LIEUTENANT (IRE) *MFMorris,Ireland* 7-11-4 DavyRussell	9/2	2½	2
4055[2]	CALL THE POLICE (IRE) *WPMullins,Ireland* 9-11-4 PaulTownend	20/1	11	3
3281*	Grands Crus (FR) *DavidPipe* 7-11-4 (t) TomScudamore	5/4 6/5f	4½	4
4121[4]	Walkon (FR) *AlanKing* 7-11-4 RobertThornton	25/1	nk	5
4055[3]	Lambro (IRE) *WPMullins,Ireland* 7-11-4 DJCasey	25/1	12	6
4141	Mr Moonshine (IRE) *SueSmith* 8-11-4 ShaneByrne	66/1	7	7
4142*	Cannington Brook (IRE) *ColinTizzard* 8-11-4 JoeTizzard	33/1	19	8
3040*	Join Together (IRE) *PaulNicholls* 7-11-4 RWalsh	7/1		pu

2.40race The Not Afraid Partnership 9ran 6m08.00

After last year's motley bunch, this race was back to what it should be, a championship race for prospective Gold Cup horses, and in the first and second 2 definite contenders for top honours emerged, their performances well up to standard for the race, and even though the favourite wasn't at his best and the likes of Last Instalment and Invictus (who had beaten the first 2 in their respective trials last time) were missing, it shouldn't be assumed they would have beaten the principals here, both clearly improved and both successful at this meeting in 2011; the pace was fair, increasing on the second circuit, the race really taking shape on the run to 3 out. **Bobs Worth**, on his toes, was a completely different proposition, with his jumping together, soon getting into a good rhythm and always comfortable with the pace, disputing after 4 out and gradually getting the better of the runner-up in the straight, just the stouter stayer at the end, not surprising given his win in the Spa Hurdle in 2011; he's had just 4 starts over fences and only just finding his stride at this discipline, so must merit serious consideration as a Gold Cup prospect next season, with the longer trip likely to be all to his advantage, a return in the Hennessy perhaps the ideal starting point; he has an excellent attitude and looks very solid and straightforward, which will stand him in good stead. **First Lieutenant**, who took the eye, improved markedly over hurdles when winning the Baring Bingham last year and did so as a chaser returned to the Festival, this his best performance in either sphere, a better round of jumping a feature of his effort and travelling well close up, drawing clear with the winner in the straight and still every chance at the last, just denied by a superior stayer; both first and second have the potential to go on and be competitive at the highest level next season, and while First Lieutenant is likely to stay beyond 3m, he might be as effective around 2½m, in which case the Ryanair could be the best target in 2013. **Call The Police** has quickly made into a smart chaser and acquitted himself well given his lack of experience over fences, jumping soundly and travelling smoothly waited with, ridden and soon no impression after 3 out but keeping on steadily; he'll presumably have the Powers Gold Cup or a race at Punchestown as his next target. **Grands Crus**, who was only confirmed earlier in the week for this in preference to a Gold Cup bid, clearly failed to run up to expectations, the manner in which he folded after improving to have every chance into the straight suggesting that something may have been amiss with him, his jumping hard to fault, as he raced relatively settled in rear; he's clearly worth the chance to bounce back and he may well show his true colours if taking his chance at Aintree, while longer term he should make an impact in open company, particularly over shorter distances, his excellent strike rate at 3m achieved almost despite the trip. **Walkon** shaped as if there may yet be a better performance in him over fences and he could be the sort for the Paddy Power in the autumn, though a novice at Aintree may be on the agenda first; he travelled well held up and jumped fluently, challenging 3 out but left behind thereafter, leaving the impression the 3m may have stretched him. **Lambro** needed to improve but still might have been expected to make more impact back at 3m, possibly finding the ground firmer than ideal, pushed along at the fifteenth and making no impression, looking rather awkward under pressure. **Mr Moonshine** continues to be highly tried over fences and shaped better than the distances suggest, just nowhere near up to the task and, though earning credit for sticking to his task under pressure from the fourteenth, having to give way after a mistake 3 out. **Cannington Brook** surely needs much more testing conditions to be seen to best advantage, never looking comfortable after a mistake at the seventh, soon losing his prominent position. **Join Together** was pulled up at this meeting for the second year running, perhaps his form last time not all it appeared, perhaps the ground a factor too, though the way he folded after a mistake at the fifteenth suggests all might not have been well either.

4609 sportingbet.com Queen Mother Champion Chase (Gr 1) (1) (5yo+) £182,240 — 2m (12)

What should have been the final fence was omitted

3794[2]	FINIAN'S RAINBOW (IRE) *NickyHenderson* 9-11-10 BarryGeraghty	9/2 4/1		1
4006[*]	SIZING EUROPE (IRE) *HenrydeBromhead,Ireland* 10-11-10 AELynch	5/6 4/5f	1¼	2
4006[2]	BIG ZEB (IRE) *ColmAMurphy,Ireland* 11-11-10 RobbiePower	6 13/2	15	3
4133[3]	Gauvain (GER) *NickWilliams* 10-11-10 (b) NoelFehily	20/1	11	4
264[2]	Realt Dubh (IRE) *NoelMeade,Ireland* 8-11-10 PaulCarberry	16 14/1	2¼	5
4116[3]	I'm So Lucky *DavidPipe* 10-11-10 (b+t) TomScudamore	66/1	10	6
4133	Kauto Stone (FR) *PaulNicholls* 6-11-10 RWalsh	14/1		1
3794[6]	Wishfull Thinking *PhilipHobbs* 9-11-10 (t) RichardJohnson	16/1		1

3.20race Mr Michael Buckley 8ran 3m52.00

There has been a general lack of depth at the top-end of this 2m division in the 2011/12 season, highlighted as well as anything by the relatively small field for a championship event, but a positive view can be taken of the first 2 given that they dominated, having it between them from a long way out, and they've both shown form above the recent standard for a Champion Chase winner—there is, however, the unusual prospect of neither ending the season as the highest rated 2m chaser, after Sprinter Sacre's outstanding performance in the Arkle; it seemed to be a truly-run affair even though the leader, Wishfull Thinking, crashed out at the fourth, a fall that led to the final fence being omitted—this inconvenienced Sizing Europe in particular but it would be stretching it to say that it definitely cost him the race. **Finian's Rainbow** might have his work cut out to retain this crown next season given how his stablemate Sprinter Sacre has burst on to the scene, but he's a good Champion Chase winner in his own right, getting the better of an on-song Sizing Europe, which takes some doing, and it was a fairly polished performance all-round; there was a change of tactics after his defeat in the Victor Chandler, kept prominent but not forcing the pace, and it possibly suited as he saw things out strongly after readily drawing clear with the runner-up from 4 out, jumping really fluently and finding extra to get on top after bypassing the last; he does have form up to 21f from his novice hurdle days and, with the yard also having Sprinter Sacre, there may be a temptation to try him over a longer trip again next season, but the feeling is that around 2m will always prove ideal. **Sizing Europe** ended up with a more difficult task than when successful in this race a year earlier, up against an improving second-season chaser, and he lost absolutely nothing in defeat—there's no doubt he'll be back winning more races at the top level next season; it perhaps wasn't ideal that he was left in the lead as early as the fourth fence, though he continued to travel and jump most exuberantly, and it was only after the bypassed-last that he had no more to give, his chances not helped by having to make the late switch from the inside, though the manoeuvre probably didn't cost him the race. **Big Zeb** would have been more of a match for the first 2 if he'd have been at the top of his game, but he hasn't been at that level on either of his last 2 starts, as far behind Sizing Europe here as at Leopardstown last month, and it was as far out as the fourth last that he looked beaten. **Gauvain** has never been up to competing at the highest level, and it was no surprise that he could make no impression; he wore blinkers for the first time since April 2009, incidentally. **Realt Dubh** has missed the majority of this season with injury, off 10 months since runner-up to Captain Chris at Punchestown, and it's probably best to forgive this given it was such a tough race to return in. **I'm So Lucky**'s efforts in the Victor Chandler and Game Spirit suggested that he wasn't a complete no-hoper, at least for place purposes, but he failed to land any sort of blow. **Kauto Stone** got no further than the first. **Wishfull Thinking**'s season has been a disappointment and a nasty-looking fall at the fourth here caps it off.

4612 Weatherbys Champion Bumper (Standard Open NHF) (Gr 1) (1) (4, 5 and 6yo) £31,323 — 2m110y

3836*	CHAMPAGNE FEVER (IRE) *WPMullins,Ireland* 5-11-5 MrPWMullins	14 16/1		1
4173*	NEW YEAR'S EVE *JohnFerguson* 4-10-11 BarryGeraghty	4 9/2f	1¼	2
4059*	PIQUE SOUS (FR) *WPMullins,Ireland* 5-11-5 RWalsh	12/1	hd	3
3891*	Moscow Mannon (IRE) *BRHamilton,Ireland* 6-11-5 MrDLavery.	13/2 8/1	4	4
2253*	Yes Way Hosay (IRE) *RoyWilson,Ireland* 6-11-5 BryanJCooper	50/1	½	5
3481*	The New One (IRE) *NigelTwiston-Davies* 4-10-11 SamTwiston-Davies	12/1	ns	6
4335*	The Romford Pele (IRE) *RebeccaCurtis* 5-11-5 APMcCoy	33/1	5	7
4432*	Jezki (IRE) *MrsJHarrington,Ireland* 4-10-11 RobbiePower	12/1	¾	8
4200*	Many Clouds (IRE) *OliverSherwood* 5-11-5 LeightonAspell	40/1	3	9
4136*	Royal Guardsman (IRE) *ColinTizzard* 5-11-5 JoeTizzard	8 6/1	1½	10
2119*	Sir Johnson *PeterBowen* 6-11-5 JamieMoore	10 7/1	2	11
4044*	Clonbanan Lad (IRE) *MichaelJohnO'Connor,Ireland* 6-11-5 MrMJO'Connor	14/1	3¾	12
4122[2]	Village Vic (IRE) *PhilipHobbs* 5-11-5 TomO'Brien	14/1	¾	13
2329*	Circular Quay *WarrenGreatrex* 5-11-5 PaddyBrennan	40/1	2¼	14
4122[3]	Horatio Hornblower (IRE) *NickWilliams* 4-10-11 JamesReveley.	14 12/1	1¾	15
4122	Piano Concerto (USA) *AndyTurnell* 5-11-5 NickScholfield	125/1	6	16
4272*	Virginia Ash (IRE) *ColinTizzard* 4-10-11 AidanColeman	50/1	nk	17
3139[4]	Ifandbutwhynot (IRE) *DavidO'Meara* 6-11-5 DenisO'Regan	50/1	nk	18
4025[3]	Glenwood Present (IRE) *BobBuckler* 5-11-5 (t) NathanSweeney	150/1		pu
3488*	Cool George *JackieduPlessis* 4-10-11 JamesBest	25/1		pu

5.15race Mrs S. Ricci 20ran 3m46.20

This looked an open renewal on form of the season's top bumper and provided a proper test, with the pace a true one, stamina coming to the fore in the end, the winner outstaying his rivals after looking third best into the straight; the Irish-trained runners regained their usual dominance after 2 years of British success, with a relatively small team including 4 of the first 5 home (the field overall was, surprisingly, below the maximum for the race), and plenty of these should make an impact over jumps next season, the form looking up to standard for the race; Patrick Mullins, winning the race for the second time, and the rider of Moscow Mannon both received bans due to their misuse of the whip. **Champagne Fever**, who looked in a bit better nick than most of his stable companions at this meeting, showed marked improvement, under a well-judged if over-forceful ride, taking it up after 1f and making the rest, racing exuberantly, and although flat out into the straight his stamina came into play and he drew away near the finish; he has the scope to make a jumper, while his pedigree and manner of racing suggest he will be at his best over further than 2m. **New Year's Eve** was all the rage ante post for this and narrowly failed to land the gamble, looking all over the winner as he made good progress 3f out and still when he put in a strong challenge in the straight but just outstayed towards the finish; he's clearly a smart prospect and should do well, whether sent novice hurdling next season or even if trained for the Flat proper. **Pique Sous** has progressed well in bumpers and showed marked improvement in this much stronger race, taking a good hold waited with and impressing with the way he travelled, well placed into the straight but unable to quicken in the final 1f. **Moscow Mannon** looks a stout stayer and these conditions were just a shade quicker than ideal for him to show to full advantage, racing prominently but tapped for foot into the straight, and although keeping on well at the finish he was unable to make an impression on the principals; he looks the part for jumping and should do well next season. **Yes Way Hosay** really looks the part for jumping, a chaser more than a hurdler, and he could well be an interesting horse to follow in that sphere next season, still looking in need of experience as he was asked for his effort down the hill but getting the hang of things into the straight and staying on well to the finish, bred to stay at least 3m over jumps. **The New One** ran well, suited by the step up to 2m and showing abundant stamina after getting tapped for foot 3f out, staying on well under pressure at the finish; he's bred for jumping and likely to make a useful novice hurdler in the autumn. **The Romford Pele** got a never-say-die McCoy ride, staying on well from a hopeless position after 4f out, appearing to show quite a bit of improvement but possibly flattered in passing beaten horses late on. **Jezki** ran respectably, though his finishing effort left a little to be desired, ridden and no extra 2f out after travelling well and weaving his way through the field down the hill; his pedigree if not his physique suggest a future as a jumper, and hopefully he'll take after his half-brother Jetson, rather than some of his other siblings, in terms of how much he finds off the bridle, this effort raising a little concern in that regard. **Many Clouds** ran creditably, given his lack of experience, tending to hang left and unable to quicken into the straight but showing enough to think he'll win a race or 2 over hurdles, likely to be suited by further than 2m in that sphere. **Royal Guardsman** ran a fair bit better than the result indicates and remains a useful prospect for hurdling next season, going well waited with at the top of the hill but carried back by a weakening runner on the rail and having to work to try and recover ground, the effort telling 2f out. **Sir Johnson** was well backed and looked to have solid form claims, his race at Aintree having worked out well, but his stable continues to struggle and he was well below his best, well positioned on the inside but clearly in trouble over 5f out and tending to hang right as he weakened; this plainly wasn't his running and as the winner of 4 bumpers he should have obvious potential as a hurdler, though it should be pointed out that runners from this stable seldom jump well enough to make an impact in their early starts over hurdles. **Clonbanan Lad** had won over 19f under testing conditions last time, so it was no real surprise he found this test against him, well placed at the top of the hill but gradually outpaced towards the straight, his rider accepting things in the final 1f; he's an athletic sort and has the potential to win races over jumps down the line, his age and pointing background suggesting chasing sooner rather than later. **Village Vic** failed to take the eye beforehand and gave the firm impression he'd left his race at Newbury, that demanding race less than a month previously; he was never in the hunt and was behind 4f out. **Circular Quay** had a fair bit to find on his debut form and made little impression on much firmer going and after a 4-month break. **Horatio Hornblower** had had quite a hard race at Newbury and looked as if he'd gone back for it, performing well below that level as well, doing too much up with the pace and weakening before the straight. **Piano Concerto** has one run that stands out among his efforts, that not likely to make him competitive at this level anyway, though it came on much softer ground than pertained here. **Virginia Ash** was behind 4f out and finishing tailed off. **Ifandbutwhynot** was possibly amiss, making a promising enough move down the hill but unable to sustain it, dropping right away. **Glenwood Present** looked out of his depth, predictably. **Cool George** was in touch until pulled up sharply over 3f out (reported to have lost his action).

CHELTENHAM Thursday, Mar 15
GOOD (New Course)

4620 Jewson Nov Chase (Golden Miller) (Gr 2) (1) (5yo+) £51,255 — 2½m (16)

Last run		Horse / Trainer / Age-Wt / Jockey		SP	Dist	Pos
3928	*	SIR DES CHAMPS (FR) *WPMullins,Ireland* 6-11-4 DavyRussell	7/2	3/1		1
3476	*	CHAMPION COURT (IRE) *MartinKeighley* 7-11-4 AlainCawley....	9	8/1	4½	2
4121	*	FOR NON STOP (IRE) *NickWilliams* 7-11-4 NoelFehily................	7	8/1	9	3
4121	2	Micheal Flips (IRE) *AndyTurnell* 8-11-4 NickScholfield.................		33/1	7	4
4270	2	Duke of Lucca (IRE) *PhilipHobbs* 7-11-4 (t) RichardJohnson........		50/1	14	5
3476	2	Solix (FR) *NickyHenderson* 6-11-4 BarryGeraghty	8	7/1	5	6
4270	ur	Zaynar (FR) *DavidPipe* 7-11-4 (b) TomScudamore....................	14	16/1	11	7
3340	2	Peddlers Cross (IRE) *DonaldMcCain* 7-11-4 JasonMaguire...........		5/2f	22	8
4270	*	Cristal Bonus (FR) *PaulNicholls* 6-11-4 RWalsh	6	13/2		pu
4393	*	Red Tanber (IRE) *BruceMactaggart* 9-11-4 LucyAlexander.........		100/1		pu

1.30race Gigginstown House Stud 10ran 4m51.60

The second running of this race, a Grade 2 novice with Grade 1 conditions and prize money, and it saw a winning performance even better than that produced by Bobs Worth in the RSA Chase the previous day; even if Sir des Champs didn't face quite the same quality of opposition, particularly with several of the more fancied contenders running well below expectations, he looks every inch a future champion; the pace was good. **Sir des Champs** maintained his unbeaten record and gained a second win at the Festival in the style of one that will go right to the top as a chaser, impressing with the way he travelled waited with in a well-run race and the turn of foot he showed to see off the resolute runner-up after the last, plenty left at the line, his jumping very solid too; while he's clearly fully effective at this trip, he will stay well and it is no surprise that he's being talked of as a prospective Gold Cup contender in 2013, sure to win more races before that comes around. **Champion Court** goes well on this track and ran his best race yet, given an attacking ride again, jumping fluently leading or disputing and really pressing on 4 out, headed and outpaced only after the last; he is a likeable sort and could well make an impact in the good handicaps here in the autumn. **For Non Stop** was a bit below his best, this perhaps not his track, his jumping okay but no better (mistake third), making headway 4 out but ridden after the next and unable to make any further impression; he's got some good efforts to his name but he's not the easiest to win with and he probably won't be easy to place once out of novice company. **Micheal Flips** was below the form he showed on his last 2 starts, though he jumped soundly in third for a long way, the effort of chasing the pace rather telling from 3 out. **Duke of Lucca**, on his toes and tongue tied, wasn't likely to be good enough and never really got on terms; he's essentially an underachiever and may struggle to make a mark out of novice company. **Solix** was closely matched with the runner-up on their showing here last time but he failed to run near that effort, his jumping not standing up nearly so well over these fences again, well back when he blundered 4 out; his future depends on getting his jumping together, likely to be found out in good handicap company if he can't do better than he did here. **Zaynar**, who has changed yards again, had blinkers back on but was a long way below his best, weakening 4 out after disputing the running; his previous trainer won a Grade 2 novice with him but, given Zaynar's attitude, his new one may well have his work cut out to add to that. **Peddlers Cross**, who reportedly suffered a muscle injury last time, was running here in preference to the Arkle and disappointed badly, ridden more patiently back at a longer trip and already struggling when blundering 4 out; he's reportedly to return to hurdling next season, when at his best he would clearly be a major contender for top honours, but he's got plenty to prove after this. **Cristal Bonus**, on his toes beforehand, ran as if all wasn't well, never travelling held up and well behind when pulled up 4 out. **Red Tanber** was out of his depth.

4622 Ryanair Chase (Festival) (Gr 1) (1) (5yo+) £148,070 2m5f (17)

Form	Horse / Trainer / Age-Weight / Jockey	Odds	Distance	Place
4133*	RIVERSIDE THEATRE *NickyHenderson* 8-11-10 BarryGeraghty ..	7/2f		1
2087*	ALBERTAS RUN (IRE) *JonjoO'Neill* 11-11-10 APMcCoy 8	10/1	½	2
4133[2]	MEDERMIT (FR) *AlanKing* 8-11-10 RobertThornton	8/1	½	3
3908[pu]	Captain Chris (IRE) *PhilipHobbs* 8-11-10 (t) RichardJohnson 9	10/1	5	4
4153*	Rubi Light (FR) *RobertHennessy,Ireland* 7-11-10 AELynch......... 8	13/2	1½	5
3794[4]	Forpadydeplasterer (IRE) *ThomasCooper,Ireland* 10-11-10 (s) BryanJCooper	40/1	8	6
3794*	Somersby (IRE) *HenriettaKnight* 8-11-10 (s) DominicElsworth... 11/2	5/1	1½	7
3043	Great Endeavour (IRE) *DavidPipe* 8-11-10 TimmyMurphy 11	12/1	19	8
2612[pu]	Kalahari King (FR) *FerdyMurphy* 11-11-10 NoelFehily	40/1	11	9
4133[pu]	Little Josh (IRE) *NigelTwiston-Davies* 10-11-10 SamTwiston-Davies	66/1	6	10
3832[2]	Noble Prince (GER) *PaulNolan,Ireland* 8-11-10 (t) DavyRussell	8/1		pu
3832*	Blazing Tempo (IRE) *WPMullins,Ireland* 8-11-3 RWalsh............ 20	16/1		pu

2.40race Jimmy Nesbitt Partnership 12ran 5m09.10

There could be no better advert for top-class horse racing than this magnificent contest, the race attracting a competitive field, well up to Grade 1 standard, the pace sound, providing a thorough examination of jumping, resolution and ability, and the finish exhilarating, with jockeyship of outstanding merit enabling the favourite to prevail, both Geraghty and McCoy on the runner-up using all their strength and skill within the new whip guidelines to get the best out of their mounts. **Riverside Theatre** gained a third successive Grade 1 victory, though he was all out to prevail and didn't run quite to his best, a couple of early mistakes making it tough for him, off the bridle a fair way from home but getting into contention with a good jump 4 out, his rider (outstanding) never letting up, ridden after 2 out and getting to the front under strong pressure close home; he's had a tough race but should continue to be a major contender in the top races, with the King George, in which he was second last season, likely to be the main aim later in the year. **Albertas Run**, patchy in his coat having been off with strained ligaments since the autumn, went agonisingly close to gaining a third win in this race, seeing off all those that challenged him for the lead under a really attacking ride from McCoy but just worn down near the finish, better than ever in defeat, having a hard race but likely to give another good account back at Aintree next month, having been first and second in the last 2 runnings of the Melling Chase. **Medermit** is thoroughly likeable, tough and consistent, and he ran his heart out again, flat to the boards at the top of the hill but responding really well to have every chance 2 out, not so fluent as the first 2 at the last and unable to finish quite so strongly as they did, racing apart from them; he was considered for the Gold Cup as an alternative and presumably connections will try 3m at some point, perhaps at Aintree or Punchestown, his merit at this trip well established, though there is a doubt on pedigree that he will stay. **Captain Chris** was much more himself, in form terms at least, though a tendency to jump right and less fluently than many cost him to a large extent, getting well back before 3 out as a result, and although he produced a strong finish he couldn't reach the principals; he won at the Punchestown Festival last spring and a return there for the Gold Cup could be the best option, with the step back up to 3m and a right-handed track both likely to benefit him. **Rubi Light**, who took the eye beforehand, ran to a similar level as when a close third in this in 2011, a little too involved in the battle for the lead, still with every chance 3 out but making a mistake there and one paced after; apart from the Melling at Aintree, there isn't an obvious race for him for the rest of the campaign, unless connections are tempted by another go at around 3m in the Punchestown Gold Cup, a race with a habit of throwing up odd results. **Forpadydeplasterer** ran as well as he's able these days, not far away before 2 out after being waited with but no impression, just not good enough anymore at this level. **Somersby** looked to have plenty going for him but disappointed, the cheekpieces not working nearly so well a second time and his effort raising serious questions about his application in what was a very attritional race, looking to be going better than many down the hill waited with but tending to edge left when shaken up and keeping plenty to himself; he's been placed on all 3 visits to Aintree and may well run a better race in the Melling if he goes there next month, perhaps with blinkers tried. **Great Endeavour** couldn't bridge the gap from top handicaps to Grade 1 company, close to the pace but quickly losing his position when he hit the thirteenth and no chance after. **Kalahari King**, runner-up in this race last year, didn't take the eye beforehand on his first start since November and didn't run much of a race, held up in rear and flat out soon after halfway, never looking likely to make an impression; he's in the veteran stage and his chances of success at this level are surely slim. **Little Josh** faced a stiff task in this company and dropped away 4 out after racing close to the pace as usual; he's been campaigned a little out of his class this season but there have been signs he retains his ability, particularly on his reappearance, and it wouldn't be a surprise to see him give a bold show if sent for the Topham and a return to handicap company next month. **Noble Prince**, on his toes and tongue tied, had won the Golden Miller at last year's Festival, and though he needed to improve on his efforts since to figure in this company he never looked likely to run near form, soon behind and pulled up at the tenth, leaving the impression he just wasn't right. **Blazing Tempo** seemed to take little interest after a slow jump at the first and eventually pulled up at the tenth.

4623 Ladbrokes World Hdle (Gr 1) (1) (4yo+) £148,070 — 3m (12)

3910*	BIG BUCK'S (FR) *PaulNicholls* 9-11-10 RWalsh	4/5 5/6f		1
3886[2]	VOLER LA VEDETTE (IRE) *ColmAMurphy,Ireland* 8-11-3 (t) AELynch	20/1	1¾	2
4134[2]	SMAD PLACE (FR) *AlanKing* 5-11-10 RobertThornton	20/1	7	3
3943[3]	Thousand Stars (FR) *WPMullins,Ireland* 8-11-10 PaulTownend	8/1	3	4
4030*	Oscar Whisky (IRE) *NickyHenderson* 7-11-10 BarryGeraghty	4/1	1½	5
4175*	Mourad (IRE) *WPMullins,Ireland* 7-11-10 MsKWalsh	33/1	26	6
4139[2]	Cross Kennon (IRE) *JennieCandlish* 8-11-10 (s) AlanO'Keeffe	100/1	3¾	7
3910[2]	Dynaste (FR) *DavidPipe* 6-11-10 (t) TomScudamore	16 14/1	1¾	8
3709*	So Young (FR) *WPMullins,Ireland* 6-11-10 DJCasey	16/1	21	9
3910[6]	Five Dream (FR) *PaulNicholls* 8-11-10 RyanMahon	100/1	49	10
4175[2]	Mikael d'Haguenet (FR) *WPMullins,Ireland* 8-11-10 DavyCondon	50/1		pu

3.20race The Stewart Family 11ran 5m43.60

A few new faces took their chance against Big Buck's in this year's World Hurdle, such as Oscar Whisky and Thousand Stars who both have top form at shorter, whilst Smad Place, Voler La Vedette and So Young all arrived on an upward curve for their first crack at this race, but in the event it probably didn't have so much depth to it as seemed likely, several not giving their running in what was a truly-run race; the pace did slacken a bit mid-race, but they'd gone quite hard early and also pressed on again a fair way out, making for a good test of stamina, as indeed this championship staying hurdle should be. **Big Buck's** is the best staying hurdler that there's ever been, not purely in terms of the raw performances he's capable of, but his record of straight wins is becoming nothing short of amazing as it stretches on, unbeaten in this sphere for over 3 years now, taking in a valuable handicap and 15 Grade 1s/2s along the way, and he just doesn't seem to have any chinks in his armour, ultimately tough and adaptable, and this day he saw off a whole new batch of rivals in the manner that we've come to expect, suggesting that he'll continue to be immensely hard to beat; kept just behind the leaders until going on himself after 3 out, he predictably didn't last as long on the bridle as a few of the others, though as Walsh shook him up he was always responding, quickening on the run between the last 2 even with the runner-up looming, and, despite drifting both ways when challenged, pulling out more to assert, as indeed he always does;

presumably next up will be Aintree where he's been successful in each of the last 4 seasons, over fences on the first occasion. **Voler La Vedette** is much improved this season, impressive for her wins in Ireland, and this was an excellent effort in defeat, worth a lot of credit for pushing Big Buck's as hard as any in this race, travelling powerfully through from the back of the field, still on the bridle on the run to the last and doing nothing at all wrong herself after being switched to the near rail with her effort, simply up against one who is very hard to crack; she's come up short when facing Quevega in the past, most recently in the 3m Grade 1 at Punchestown last year, but if the pair meet there again this year then it will be a close run thing. **Smad Place**'s Grade 1 placing highlights the swift progress that he's made this term, ultimately coming up short for ability against the first 2, and he was well-ridden to get the most out of him, not pressing on with the principals when things began to fully develop and able to see the race out thoroughly as a result, the trip obviously within reach; he's proved consistent and has a likeable way of going about things, so should continue to give a good account. **Thousand Stars**'s French Champion Hurdle win last summer wasn't conclusive evidence of his stamina for this sort of trip, the emphasis having been firmly on speed that day due to a slow pace, and he appeared to fall short on that front here after turning into the straight on the bridle; he'll presumably go for the Aintree Hurdle again next month (beaten a neck by Oscar Whisky in it last season). **Oscar Whisky** was never sure to stay this far and blatantly found his stamina stretched, still cruising into the straight but tiring quickly, albeit having made a couple of mistakes; he's a fully proven top-class hurdler and will continue to make his presence felt at shorter trips, sure to hold leading claims if aiming to repeat his Aintree Hurdle win of last season next month. **Mourad** is a very smart hurdler who rarely fails to give his running, so presumably something wasn't right with him here, weakening rapidly after 2 out. **Cross Kennon** was flattered when fourth in this race last season (set steady pace) and weakened out of this quickly after 3 out, having been forced to do more in front this time around. **Dynaste** was oddly fitted with a tongue strap on the back of a career-best effort behind Big Bucks in the Cleeve here in January, and he made only a brief effort after the third last before weakening. **So Young** has looked good in winning lesser races, both as a novice and this season, but when he's tackled top company he's come up short, certainly so here, his performance almost too bad to be true. **Five Dream** was in a more competitive race along with Big Bucks on this occasion and found the task beyond him. **Mikael D'Haguenet** lost touch quickly after the eighth and must have been amiss.

CHELTENHAM Friday, Mar 16
GOOD (New Course)

4640 JCB Triumph Hdle (Gr 1) (1) (4yo) £56,950 2m1f (8)

4052[3]	COUNTRYWIDE FLAME *JohnQuinn* 4-11-0 DougieCostello	33/1		1
4052*	HISAABAAT (IRE) *DKWeld,Ireland* 4-11-0 AELynch	20/1	3	2
4269*	GRUMETI *AlanKing* 4-11-0 RobertThornton	6 5/1f	¾	3
4269[2]	Dodging Bullets *PaulNicholls* 4-11-0 DarylJacob	20/1	hd	4
4038[4]	Wingtips (FR) *AJMartin,Ireland* 4-11 0 BryanJCooper	100/1	4½	5
4266[2]	Sadler's Risk (IRE) *PhilipHobbs* 4-11-0 RichardJohnson	7 13/2	¾	6
3905[3]	Hollow Tree *DonaldMcCain* 4-11-0 JasonMaguire	20/1	¾	7
4052	His Excellency (IRE) *GordonElliott,Ireland* 4-11-0 DavyRussell	100/1	nk	8
4266*	Baby Mix (FR) *TomGeorge* 4-11-0 PaddyBrennan	6/1	1	9
4294*	Asaid *JohnFerguson* 4-11-0 (s) BarryGeraghty	25/1	2¼	10
4187*	Urbain de Sivola (FR) *NickWilliams* 4-11-0 NoelFehily	14/1	13	11
4052[2]	Shadow Catcher *GordonElliott,Ireland* 4-11-0 PaulCarberry	10/1	1¾	12
3926*	Darroun (IRE) *WPMullins,Ireland* 4-11-0 DJCasey	14/1	½	13
4049[5]	Arctic Reach *BrendanPowell* 4-11-0 AidanColeman	200/1	sh	14
4405*	Dysios (IRE) *DenisWCullen,Ireland* 4-11-0 TomDoyle	100/1	1¾	15
4125[3]	Mattoral *ChrisGordon* 4-11-0 (b) TomCannon	200/1	45	16
4135*	Balder Succes (FR) *AlanKing* 4-11-0 WayneHutchinson	15/2		f
3905[2]	Pearl Swan (FR) *PaulNicholls* 4-11-0 RWalsh	13/2 7/1		f
4052	Ut de Sivola (FR) *WPMullins,Ireland* 4-11-0 PaulTownend	20/1		pu
4032*	West Brit (IRE) *CharlieLongsdon* 4-11-0 (t) TomScudamore	66/1		pu

1.30race Estio Pinnacle Racing 20ran 3m58.60

A wide-open running of the top 4-y-o hurdle of the season, and loads still had a chance after 2 out, the winner tenth and flat out going nowhere turning in, the sound pace from after the first ensuring the finish was all about stamina, the winner possessing it in spades, some of the others not so much, the position of leading juvenile in so far a slightly substandard year very much still up for grabs, the fourth and the faller Balder Succes among those that might yet claim that crown at Aintree. **Countrywide Flame** has proved really tough and consistent and showed all his battling qualities to prevail, awkward round the top bend and losing his position, flat out and going nowhere 2 out before he stayed on really strongly in the straight to challenge at the last, soon in front and drawing away towards the finish, well on top at the line; this was a real test of stamina, which suited him down to the ground, and he would be far from certain to confirm placings with several of these were they to meet in the Anniversary at Aintree on anything less testing than soft ground; his longer-term future lies over further and his attitude suggests he's likely to pay his way in handicaps next season even if his mark might life hard for him in the first instance. **Hisaabaat**, surprisingly without the headgear which had seemed to help him at Leopardstown, nevertheless ran really well, given a very patient ride, weaving his way through from mid-field after travelling well to challenge at the last, perfectly ridden to beat all those in front of him into the straight, unfortunately mugged by one coming from behind him; he's smart and will win more races, the result at Leopardstown perhaps a truer reflection of the potential of the first 2 here. **Grumeti** had jumped well when winning the Dovecote but wasn't nearly so fluent here, making 2 notable mistakes which might well have been crucial, though his superiority over the runner-up at Kempton was reduced and may well be removed altogether another day; held up, he blundered at the fifth and came off the bridle briefly, worked his way to the front at the last but made another mistake and was soon headed, unable to quicken after. **Dodging Bullets**, who looked very well and was on his toes, has the potential to be the best of these, doing well given his lack of experience over hurdles, impressing with the way he travelled and looking all over the winner as he moved up after 2 out to hold every chance at the last, just short of the stamina needed for the climb to the finish; he'll hold an excellent chance of reversing placings with the trio in front of him were they to meet again at Aintree under conditions which place more emphasis on speed. **Wingtips**'s apparently much-improved effort wasn't a total surprise on Flat form, jumping better on less testing ground and probably suited by the run of the race as well, held up towards the rear and travelling well, making his effort 2 out and good progress until no extra at the last; his form on the Flat suggests he'll have no problem with a step up in trip. **Sadler's Risk** has potential yet to make a greater impact over hurdles, almost certainly when faced with a longer trip, soon setting a sound pace here but ridden after a mistake 2 out and tapped for foot when squeezed out before the last, staying on again after the last. **Hollow Tree** ran creditably, travelling smoothly close up to 2 out and trying to press on into the straight but unable to hold his position approaching the last, not good enough under the conditions, though he's a likeable type and a return to softer ground and a step up in trip may yet draw a better performance from him. **His Excellency** looked very well and ran his best race over hurdles, facing a stiff task, though he was never in contention and may well be flattered, staying on well in the closing stages. **Baby Mix** has the potential to be a smart performer but also to be very frustrating, his finishing effort, as in the Finesse, disappointing, after he'd travelled well taking a good hold behind the leaders; his physique and demeanour suggest he'll make a chaser, and a switch to that sphere may well pay dividends in the autumn. **Asaid** couldn't quite match the form he showed when fourth to Hisaabaat at Leopardstown but ran creditably, handy enough at the top of the hill but pushed along and unable to quicken after the next, essentially not good enough. **Urbain de Sivola** looked to have a solid form chance but was let down by his jumping, not fluent at times but closing when pecking 2 out and unable to recover, allowed to come home in his own time; he's clearly a fair bit better than this indicates and may show as much with a better round of jumping, with softer ground probably also likely to help him; his stable had a disappointing week, and is still without a first Festival win. **Shadow Catcher** was closely matched with the first 2 from last time but failed to give his running, dropped out last, travelling well, but still having plenty to do before 2 out and failing to pick up when ridden, his rider giving up in the end; his best form on the Flat came in the mud and, whilst it's still early days with him as a hurdler, maybe testing conditions are going to be bring the best out of him in this sphere, too. **Darroun** probably did too much early in the race, taking a good hold up with the pace, and although still with every chance 2 out he could find no extra under pressure and was eased; his earlier efforts and physique suggest there may yet be better to come from him. **Arctic Reach**, without the cheekpieces he wore in a jumpers bumper last time, faced a stiff task and wasn't able to make much impact, weakening after 2 out having tried to close down the hill. **Dysios** is an athletic sort who may well do better again back at a more suitable level, just outclassed at this one, held up in rear and asked for an effort after 3 out but making no impression. **Mattoral**, edgy beforehand, wasn't up to this class, failing to settle early and well held by 3 out. **Balder Succes** fell at the fourth. **Pearl Swan**, on his toes beforehand, is possibly just not straightforward and worth trying in headgear, as he was off the bridle in rear from an early stage, although he did begin to pick up 2 out and was staying on well when he fell at the last, likely to have finished fifth at worst, probably just behind the placed horses; he has the potential to make a smart hurdler still if his ability can be channelled correctly. **Ut de Sivola** had had an excuse for his poor effort when favourite behind the first 2 at Leopardstown and needs another here, failing to settle held up but in trouble 3 out and soon behind; he has plenty to prove if one isn't forthcoming. **West Brit** had a lot on in this company and wasn't up to the task, weakening 3 out after racing prominently.

4642 Albert Bartlett Nov Hdle (Spa) (Gr 1) (1) (4yo+) £56,950 — 3m (12)

4138-*	BRINDISI BREEZE (IRE) *LucindaRussell* 6-11-7 CampbellGillies	17/2	7/1		1
3944-*	BOSTON BOB (IRE) *WPMullins,Ireland* 7-11-7 RWalsh		6/5f	2	2
4141-*	GRAND VISION (IRE) *ColinTizzard* 6-11-7 TomO'Brien		25/1	1¼	3
4146-*	Lovcen (GER) *AlanKing* 7-11-7 RobertThornton	16	12/1	6	4
4138-3	Meister Eckhart (IRE) *RebeccaCurtis* 6-11-7 APMcCoy		22/1	½	5
3689-*	The Druids Nephew (IRE) *AndyTurnell* 5-11-7 NickScholfield		100/1	8	6
3181-2	Mount Benbulben (IRE) *GordonElliott,Ireland* 7-11-7 PaulCarberry	9	11/1	1¾	7
3916-*	Rocky Creek (IRE) *PaulNicholls* 6-11-7 DarylJacob	12	14/1	7	8
3765-*	Fox Appeal (IRE) *EmmaLavelle* 5-11-7 NoelFehily	20	18/1	½	9
4141-pu	Tour des Champs (FR) *NigelTwiston-Davies* 5-11-7 SamTwiston-Davies		150/1	¾	10
3911-4	Sivola de Sivola (FR) *TomGeorge* 6-11-7 PaddyBrennan	18	16/1	17	11
4160-2	Benheir (IRE) *RebeccaCurtis* 6-11-7 AidanColeman		100/1	1¾	12
4333-2	Dawn Commander (GER) *CharlieLongsdon* 5-11-7 RichardJohnson		66/1	19	13
4181-*	Big Occasion (IRE) *DavidPipe* 5-11-7 (b) TomScudamore		50/1	5	14
3944-5	Sea of Thunder (IRE) *CharlesByrnes,Ireland* 7-11-7 DavyRussell	10	9/1	¾	15
4273-4	Fill The Power (IRE) *SueSmith* 6-11-7 ShaneByrne		125/1	6	16
4025-2	Hard To Swallow (IRE) *MartinKeighley* 6-11-7 AlainCawley		33/1	4½	17
3042-3	American Spin *LukeDace* 8-11-7 TimmyMurphy		100/1		pu
3703-*	Ipsos du Berlais (FR) *NoelMeade,Ireland* 6-11-7 DavyCondon		20/1		pu
3996-*	The Bosses Cousin (IRE) *WPMullins,Ireland* 7-11-7 PaulTownend		66/1		pu

2.40race Mr Sandy Seymour 20ran 5m46.30

Nothing was able to match the performance of Simonsig in the Baring Bingham, but it was a decent renewal of this race nonetheless, with the first 3 running to the level of an average winner; a sound pace was disputed by Big Occasion and Brindisi Breeze, making for a thorough test on watered ground, and the result on the whole looks a solid one. **Brindisi Breeze** has stepped up to the mark on each rise in class, up against the pick of the staying novices this time and improving further to see them all off under a typically aggressive ride, certainly proving himself a lot more than a mudlark, potentially a high-class stayer, and he's very much one to look forward to if sent chasing next season—he is a point winner and his style is that of one that should do really well over fences. **Boston Bob** met with his first defeat over hurdles but remains a top prospect, hugely impressive for all of his wins in Ireland and, although he couldn't quite match his previous 2 performances here, it was still a very good effort behind a promising rival; he didn't travel particularly well, in part due to a couple of less-than-fluent jumps, whilst conditions were also less testing than he'd faced this season, but his response to pressure was hard to knock, chasing the winner down from 2 out and looking to have a chance until the final 150 yards; he has the size for chasing and that's presumably the plan for next season. **Grand Vision**'s easy Haydock win is proving strong form, with 3 Festival winners in behind him that day, and this represents further significant improvement on his part, always in touch and sticking to his task well having come under pressure before the second last; he has filling out to do and both size and pedigree suggest that he'll make at least as good a chaser. **Lovcen** found the task beyond him, unable to improve further and never a serious threat, though still matching the form of his handicap win last month, the trip no problem as anticipated. **Meister Eckhart** was third to Brindisi Breeze at Haydock and that form is clearly better than it looked at the time, shaping even better here than the result in fact, travelling and jumping fluently close up and tiring only after turning into the straight in second; he'd be one to consider if turning up at Aintree for the Sefton Novices' Hurdle next month. **The Druids Nephew** was always likely to struggle taking such a big step up in class but showed himself to be a useful novice and might have finished closer but for being tight for room on the turn towards 2 out, ending up with more to do than ideal and staying on without being unduly knocked about; it's early days and he may prove capable of better still. **Mount Benbulben**, a good sort who took the eye beforehand, failed to meet expectations on the day, going rather freely and not proving so well suited by the trip as seemed likely; there are a lot of positives to take from this season as a whole and he's not one to be writing off, be it kept over hurdles or sent chasing. **Rocky Creek** is still a very inexperienced horse and may not have been ready for such a tough assignment, faced with a big field in a Grade 1, and he seemed out of his comfort zone from an early stage; his Doncaster form is solid and there's plenty of time for him still to progress, with chasing the obvious route for next season, a useful-looker who is bred for it. **Fox Appeal**'s most recent Taunton win was impressive, but the form hasn't worked out, and he struggled up in class here, losing his place after clouting the third last. **Tour des Champs** is more a handicapper, this level beyond him, and the headway that he made was only late on through tiring rivals. **Sivola de Sivola** was off the bridle from an early stage and, whilst he's generally held his form this season, this was a slightly worrying display with the future in mind. **Benheir** faced a stiff task and was struggling by 3 out. **Dawn Commander** is of some interest for handicaps after his second at Bangor, but he was punching above his weight here. **Big Occasion** won't be the easiest to place from now on, not good enough for this sort of level, high enough in the weights for handicaps and under a double-penalty in any ordinary novice. **Sea of Thunder** shaped as if amiss, travelling okay until before 2 out but beaten in a matter of strides. **Fill The Power** was out of his depth and never travelled. **Hard To Swallow** has had his sights set high all season, showing enough previously to win a normal novice hurdle, but the way that he hung as he weakened here was a little disconcerting. **American Spin** seems no better than fairly useful, so this was asking far too much. **Ipsos du Berlais** has done well in the mud in Ireland and the less testing ground here was possibly against him, though it could be something went wrong with him. **The Bosses Cousin**'s effort is best ignored, out of his depth and also not seeming right, and he remains with potential at a lower level.

4643 Betfred Cheltenham Gold Cup Chase (Gr 1) (1) (5yo+) £284,750 — 3¼m110y (22)

3382 *	SYNCHRONISED (IRE) *JonjoO'Neill* 9-11-10 APMcCoy	15/2 8/1		1
4117 4	THE GIANT BOLSTER *DavidBridgwater* 7-11-10 TomScudamore	50/1	2¼	2
4117 *	LONG RUN (FR) *NickyHenderson* 7-11-10 MrSWaley-Cohen	2 7/4f	¾	3
4117 2	Burton Port (IRE) *NickyHenderson* 8-11-10 BarryGeraghty	13/2 8/1	5	4
3908 4	Time For Rupert (IRE) *PaulWebber* 8-11-10 DenisO'Regan	33/1	1½	5
4072 2	Knockara Beau (IRE) *GeorgeCharlton* 9-11-10 JanFaltejsek	66/1	10	6
3908 *	Midnight Chase *NeilMulholland* 10-11-10 DougieCostello	12/1	11	7
4057 5	China Rock (IRE) *MFMorris,Ireland* 9-11-10 AELynch	100/1	17	8
3993 3	The Midnight Club (IRE) *WPMullins,Ireland* 11-11-10 PaulTownend	100/1	15	9
3335 pu	Carruthers *MarkBradstock* 9-11-10 (t) MattieBatchelor	100/1	7	10
4117 3	What A Friend *PaulNicholls* 9-11-10 (b) DarylJacob	25/1		f
3908 5	Diamond Harry *NickWilliams* 9-11-10 NoelFehily	20/1		pu
3283 *	Kauto Star (FR) *PaulNicholls* 12-11-10 (t) RWalsh	4 3/1		pu
2621 3	Weird Al (IRE) *DonaldMcCain* 9-11-10 JasonMaguire	8/1		pu

3.20race Mr John P. McManus 14ran 6m34.80

A race so long anticipated can seldom have proved such a let-down on the day, the decider between Kauto Star and Long Run deciding nothing, the former clearly not himself and pulled up on the first circuit, the latter nothing like the horse he was earlier in the season, let alone last; several among the more likely to take advantage if that pair came up short also failed to deliver and the form is clearly well below the recent standard for the race, the winner somewhat flattered in picking up the pieces off a good gallop, the fifth shaping like the best horse on the day before his exertions told going to the last—all in all an unsatisfactory race, with the principals decidedly vulnerable in future to the pick of the season's novices, Sir des Champs, Bobs Worth and Last Instalment not least among them. **Synchronised**, while obviously capable of a very high level of form, was surely flattered by the result here, for seldom can a Gold Cup winner have jumped so indifferently or travelled less well, held up as usual and his abundant stamina kicking in late on after he'd been on and off the bridle from before halfway; this will surely be the pinnacle of his career, the Grand National under top weight a task that he most likely won't be up to, and next year's Gold Cup against some of the up-and-coming chasers seen at this meeting likely to be a tougher challenge; his success was a notable one for his sire Sadler's Wells, the pre-eminent Flat sire and incidental sire of good hurdlers, notably Istabraq. **The Giant Bolster** excelled himself, given a more patient ride than has been the case of late and showed more stamina than he had last time over 3m, produced to challenge after 4 out and leading in the straight but headed and one pace after the last; he's confirmed himself a high-class chaser, one that jumps much better these days, and while he won't be the easiest to place after this he is genuine and young enough to improve a little further. **Long Run**, the pick of the paddock, just wasn't at his best for no obvious reason; waited with in touch and poised to challenge after 4 out, he made a mistake at the next which didn't help his cause but his jumping wasn't the cause of his defeat, still every chance at the last, just one paced under pressure; he remains the most likely in this field to win a Gold Cup in the future and is young enough to return in top form next season. **Burton Port** looked in good shape but didn't make quite the progress anticipated from Newbury, a little flat, rather as he had been in the RSA Chase in 2010, under pressure for most of the final circuit, perhaps a flatter track suiting him ideally; he holds a Grand National entry, and makes some appeal for that task, though presumably the Bowl is an alternative option. **Time For Rupert** shaped a lot better than he has for much of the season, jumping well up with the pace and still travelling smoothly in front after 3 out but then finding his earlier exertions telling, weakening out of the frame at the last; he was a top-class hurdler in his prime and there might yet be better to come over fences, with the Grand National an option in future seasons; he was reportedly treated for heat exhuastion but was said to be fine. **Knockara Beau** has a solid record here over the years and ran about as well as he's able in face of a stiff task, sticking to his task well having been well out of contention 4 out; he's often highly tried, and as a result wins infrequently. **Midnight Chase** essentially isn't up to the standard required at this level, running well below the form he showed when fifth in last year's renewal, this not an ideal race in which to try and make all, uncharacteristic mistakes creeping in in the last 1m, dropping right away after another one 4 out and then short of room; he has an entry in the Grand National, and his style of racing and sound jumping could well see him take to that unique course. **China Rock** was running well when going wrong in this race last year and again shaped well for a long way, still in touch 3 out before lack of stamina told, tying up quite badly in the closing stages; the programme in Ireland provides opportunities for a horse of his ability, so there may be more races at a lower level to be won with him. **The Midnight Club**, yet another from his yard that failed to take the eye during the meeting, was always behind in face of a stiff task, hampered at the second and spared a hard race; he's presumably being brought to a peak for the Grand National, a race in which he started favourite last season and finished sixth despite making mistakes. **Carruthers** was much more patiently ridden than usual but his race was effectively over very early on, hampered at the second and making a mistake at the third **What A Friend** fell at the second. **Diamond Harry** had had a breathing operation since the Argento but to no beneficial effect at the first attempt, labouring from a long way out having been held up off the pace; he couldn't be backed with confidence if turned out again this season. **Kauto Star**, on what will surely be his swansong, was pulled up after the ninth, having jumped off with the leaders but lost his position after the sixth; he'd had a well-publicised fall in training 2 weeks before the race and that may well have had an impact on his performance here, his final appearance, like that of the great hurdler Istabraq, one of anti-climax; he deserves to be long remembered for his exploits as a chaser, a superb jumper at his best, with a level of ability unsurpassed in the last 45 years, his career notable for its longevity as well as unprecedented success, his 16 Grade 1 victories including the King George 5 times and this race twice. **Weird Al** had been well supported in the expectation that he'd be freshened up by a break since the Betfair Chase but he ran as if all wasn't well, always fragile as it is, travelling well held up to halfway but soon in trouble after and pulled up before 4 out, reported to have bled; he looks favourably weighted for the Grand National but whether he even makes the line-up must be doubted after this.

AINTREE Thursday, Apr 12
GOOD to SOFT

5132 BGC Partners Liverpool Hdle (Gr 1) (1) (4yo+) £56,736 — 3m110y (13)

Form	Horse	Odds	Dist	Pos
4623[*]	BIG BUCK'S (FR) *PaulNicholls* 9-11-7 RWalsh	1/5 2/9f		1
4624[pu]	CRACK AWAY JACK *TomGeorge* 8-11-7 (t) NoelFehily	33/1	9	2
4621[pu]	ACROSS THE BAY (IRE) *DonaldMcCain* 8-11-7 (b) JasonMaguire	50/1	3¼	3
4117[5]	Tidal Bay (IRE) *PaulNicholls* 11-11-7 NickScholfield	16 14/1	7	4
3480[2]	Poungach (FR) *PaulNicholls* 6-11-7 DarylJacob	14 12/1	3¾	5
4621	Restless Harry *RobinDickin* 8-11-7 CharliePoste	20/1		f
4623[3]	Smad Place (FR) *AlanKing* 5-11-7 RobertThornton	5/1		ur
4787[3]	Won In The Dark (IRE) *SabrinaJHarty,Ireland* 8-11-7 AELynch	33/1		bd

2.00race The Stewart Family 8ran 6m15.30

A substandard Grade 1 on bare form, some of the depth taken away by fallers (including second-favourite Smad Place), and Across The Bay's proximity means the race can't be rated highly, the outstanding Big Buck's finding it all so easy; the pace was modest and it was only from 4 out that things developed. **Big Buck's** made history, his winning streak of 17 the longest ever recorded in National Hunt racing, testament to his talent and toughness, whilst his stable deserves plenty of credit, too; in performance terms, this was a long way short of Big Bucks' best, left as he was with a simple opportunity, but he could hardly have done it any more easily, cruising to the front approaching 3 out and stretching clear between the last 2 before heavily eased; he'll continue to be extremely hard to beat next season. **Crack Away Jack**, who'd left Paul Nicholls since Cheltenham, was fitted with a tongue tie for just his second outing over hurdles since 2008/9 and showed his best form for a while, having no chance with Big Buck's but seeing things out well, the longer trip not seeming a problem; he was slightly hampered after Restless Harry's fall, but it made little difference. **Across The Bay** ran with credit retried in blinkers to be placed in a race which rather fell apart behind the winner, quickly bouncing back after being pulled up at Cheltenham, sticking on as best he could after headed entering the straight. **Tidal Bay** would probably have been placed but for getting hampered after Restless Harry came down at the eighth, left a long way back and staying on steadily; he's not one to be making excuses for, though. **Poungach** faced by far his stiffest task to date but was disappointing even so, prominent only until after 4 out, lack of stamina not the reason for his weakening (should stay at least 3m); it's still early days with him and he has the look of a potentially smart novice chaser next season. **Restless Harry** is generally a safe jumper but crashed out at the eighth here (brought down Won In The Dark). **Smad Place** was in a share of third when blundering and unseating 4 out. **Won In The Dark** was brought down by Restless Harry's fall at the eighth.

5134 Betfred Bowl Chase (Gr 1) (1) (5yo+) £84,405 — 3m1f (19)

Form	Horse	Odds	Dist	Pos
4545[4]	FOLLOW THE PLAN (IRE) *OliverMcKiernan,Ireland* 9-11-7 (s) TomDoyle	50/1		1
4643[4]	BURTON PORT (IRE) *NickyHenderson* 8-11-7 APMcCoy	4/1	3	2
4598[*]	HUNT BALL (IRE) *KeiranBurke* 7-11-7 NickScholfield	11/2 6/1	nk	3
4622[3]	Medermit (FR) *AlanKing* 8-11-7 RobertThornton	11/2 5/1	ns	4
4268[*]	Nacarat (FR) *TomGeorge* 11-11-7 (t) PaddyBrennan	12 10/1	4½	5
4395[*]	Master of The Hall (IRE) *NickyHenderson* 8-11-7 AndrewTinkler	20/1	4½	6
4643[f]	What A Friend *PaulNicholls* 9-11-7 (b) RWalsh	7 9/1	4½	7
4567	Roberto Goldback (IRE) *DTHughes,Ireland* 10-11-7 (v) BryanJCooper	100/1	14	8
4643	Carruthers *MarkBradstock* 9-11-7 (b+t) MattieBatchelor	25/1	27	9
4643[pu]	Diamond Harry *NickWilliams* 9-11-7 NoelFehily	14 8/1		pu
4622[*]	Riverside Theatre *NickyHenderson* 8-11-7 BarryGeraghty	7/2f		pu

3.05race Redgap Partnership 11ran 6m25.80

It is often the case in this late-season Grade 1 that some of the leading contenders flop after hard races at Cheltenham, the likes of Kauto Star, Denman and Imperial Commander all having been beaten here in recent years, and it was a similar story again as the standard-setting Riverside Theatre bombed out, whilst a few others weren't at their very best, either; Nacarat set a fair pace and there wasn't any positional advantage. **Follow The Plan** caused a big upset and seemed to benefit considerably from the fitting of blinkers for all this was his third Grade 1 win, cruising up from the back before quickening ahead between the last 2; whether the headgear has the same effect a second time remains to be seen, and the feeling is that he'll be opposable at shorter odds in next month's Guinness Gold Cup. **Burton Port**'s season has to be viewed as a success after his long absence through injury, in the frame in the Gold Cup and now runner-up in another Grade 1, the fact that he's holding his form certainly encouraging; even back on a flat track he looked hard work, however, off the bridle before the other principals and merely staying on late, and perhaps he's worth trying in a valuable long-distance handicap next season, acknowledging that it would require improvement to defy a BHA mark of 166. **Hunt Ball**'s season has been remarkable and this Grade-1 placing highlights just how far he has come in less than 6 months, taking his form to an even higher level here, the trip not a problem for all that he travelled (and jumped) as fluently as any for a long way. **Medermit** proved his stamina tried beyond 21f for the first time, so there are more options next season, likely to be campaigned for the King George to start with, and he'll be in with a shout having established himself at the top level; admittedly, this bare form doesn't match up to his very best, but he'd have been second had he not hit the third last (just as he was winding up), and overall he has a positive profile, extremely tough and consistent. **Nacarat**'s Racing Plus Chase win has taken a few knocks and, although he wasn't discredited in his bid to follow up last year's success in this race, his finishing effort was a disappointment (not for the first time) after he was headed between the last 2. **Master of The Hall** is short of this standard, his success the time before coming in a much lesser contest at Kelso, and in his own terms this was a perfectly respectable effort for all he was never a threat. **What A Friend** did make one bad mistake but his attitude seems to be getting worse if anything and, as such, is one to treat with caution, unsure to take advantage even if he's eased in class (without a win for 2 years). **Roberto Goldback**'s recent record is rather hit-and-miss and he didn't fire in a change of headgear, making little impression. **Carruthers**, in first-time blinkers, had no excuses and has simply lost his way since winning a substandard renewal of the Hennessy. **Diamond Harry** has his problems and they have really told this season, out of sorts since his reappearance, clearly amiss here as he lost his place quickly on the final circuit. **Riverside Theatre** had a tough race in the Ryanair and was presumably feeling the effects of that, not jumping or travelling well from an early stage; he's still a candidate for top honours next season.

AINTREE Friday, Apr 13
GOOD to SOFT

5148 John Smith's Melling Chase (Gr 1) (1) (5yo+) 2½m (16)
£98,557

4609*	FINIAN'S RAINBOW (IRE) *NickyHenderson* 9-11-10 BarryGeraghty	7/4 13/8f	1
4609f	WISHFULL THINKING *PhilipHobbs* 9-11-10 (t) RichardJohnson	9 15/2	7 2
4622²	ALBERTAS RUN (IRE) *JonjoO'Neill* 11-11-10 APMcCoy	9/4 11/4	13 3
4622⁶	Forpadydeplasterer (IRE) *ThomasCooper,Ireland* 10-11-10 (s) BryanJCooper	12/1	1¼ 4
4900⁶	Pure Faith (IRE) *PeterBowen* 8-11-10 TomO'Brien	80/1	6 5
3907²	Poquelin (FR) *PaulNicholls* 9-11-10 RWalsh	6 5/1	13 6
4609f	Kauto Stone (FR) *PaulNicholls* 6-11-10 PaulCarberry	12/1	½ 7
4622	Kalahari King (FR) *FerdyMurphy* 11-11-10 NoelFehily	33/1	pu

3.05race Mr Michael Buckley 8ran 5m03.40

Not masses of depth to this year's Melling Chase but the performance of Finian's Rainbow was right out of the top drawer, bettering even that of Master Minded last season; Albertas Run and Poquelin took each other on up front and ensured that matters were truly run. **Finian's Rainbow** has an outstanding record as a chaser, defeated only twice (in Grade 1s) and never out of the first 2, and this follow up to his Champion Chase win confirms everything that he achieved at Cheltenham, making just one mistake (at the tenth) and always cruising, drawing right away on the flat once nudged along; he faces the prospect of having to take on stable-companion Sprinter Sacre if dropped back to 2m next season, but he'll be no pushover himself, while there is also the option of longer trips, but 3m in the King George might stretch him. **Wishfull Thinking** bounced back to his very best from out of the blue, his nasty fall in the Champion Chase clearly not having had a lasting effect, having no chance with Finian's Rainbow but worth plenty of credit for pulling so far clear of the rest after impressing with how he moved up entering the straight. **Albertas Run** proved in the Ryanair that he retains all of his ability and, as an 11-y-o, it may be that a hard race at Cheltenham had taken more out of him than in the previous 2 years, jumping sloppily and left behind approaching 2 out. **Forpadydeplasterer** is no longer as competitive as he used to be at the top level, and yet again he failed to see things out fully, admittedly after making several mistakes. **Pure Faith** faced a very stiff task and predictably lost touch from 4 out. **Poquelin** stopped quickly having raced enthusiastically in front for a long way; he hasn't been so consistent this season, his second at Cheltenham in January a stand-out effort. **Kauto Stone** has been a disappointment since his second in the Tingle Creek, a first-fence faller in last month's Champion Chase and labouring some way out here. **Kalahari King** has totally lost his way since runner-up in last year's Ryanair.

AINTREE Saturday, Apr 14
GOOD to SOFT; National Course GOOD

5161 John Smith's Maghull Nov Chase (Gr 1) (1) (5yo+) £56,270 — 2m (12)

4593*	SPRINTER SACRE (FR) *NickyHenderson* 6-11-4 BarryGeraghty	1/6 1/7f		1
4646bd	TOUBAB (FR) *PaulNicholls* 6-11-4 RWalsh	9 10/1	13	2
4345*	KUDU COUNTRY (IRE) *TomTate* 6-11-4 JamesReveley	25/1	36	3
2394*	Australia Day (IRE) *PaulWebber* 9-11-4 DenisO'Regan	14/1	7	4

2.15race Mrs Caroline Mould 4ran 3m53.40

hree of those that dared to take their chance against outstanding novice Sprinter Sacre weren't near to the standard usually required to win at this level, so it was no surprise that the winner coasted home. **Sprinter Sacre** was in a different league to his rivals, forcing his rider to send him on at the sixth, jumping boldly in front and still coasting when left with a bigger advantage 2 out, any amount in hand at the finish; he's a most exciting prospect for open company next season and it's no surprise that he's already a short-priced favourite for the Champion Chase. **Toubab**'s chasing form has warranted more than 1 win in this first season, though his future prospects rest with the handicapper's view of this second to an outstanding novice who toyed with him, typically travelling strongly waited with and around 6 lengths down when hitting 2 out, his rider holding him together thereafter. **Kudu Country**, facing an impossible task against the winner, was much more patiently ridden than usual and completed in his own time for third, not fluent at the second and making a mistake at the eighth; he's best judged on his earlier efforts. **Australia Day** had won his only previous start left handed over jumps but he clearly appeared inconvenienced running that way round for the first time over fences, jumping badly right at the first (nearly running out) and continuing to do so to a lesser extent, his jumping lacking fluency in general; he's not been entirely convincing so far over fences, but it might be best to give him the benefit of the doubt if he turns up at Perth, for example, under optimum conditions later in the month.

5162 John Smith's Aintree Hdle (Gr 1) (1) (4yo+) 2½m (11)
£90,096

4623[5] OSCAR WHISKY (IRE) *NickyHenderson* 7-11-7 BarryGeraghty 11/4 9/4 1
4623[4] THOUSAND STARS (FR) *WPMullins,Ireland* 8-11-7 PaulTownend .... 6 7/1 nk 2
4595* ROCK ON RUBY (IRE) *PaulNicholls* 7-11-7 (t) NoelFehily 5/2 5 3
4610 Third Intention (IRE) *ColinTizzard* 5-11-7 (t) JoeTizzard........ 33/1 13 4
4595[5] Zarkandar (IRE) *PaulNicholls* 5-11-7 RWalsh .... 15/8 2/1f f
2.50race Walters Plant Hire Ltd 5ran 4m51.80

A smaller field than usual for this Grade 1 but it still had a lot of quality, Champion Hurdler Rock On Ruby taking on Oscar Whisky and Thousand Stars, who'd finished first and second in last year's renewal; the first-named wasn't at his best, however, and it was the same pair that fought it out again in a modestly-run affair—there was no clear front runner and they stood still for a few seconds after the tape was released. **Oscar Whisky** is a top-class hurdler with a tremendous strike-rate and he made it successive wins in this Grade 1 just over 4 weeks after blatantly failing to stay in the World Hurdle; the bare form doesn't quite match his best, but it was very similar to last year's win in that he fought off Thousand Stars in a tight finish, taking over between the last 2 and digging deep; he's well worth trying in the Champion Hurdle again next season, having finished third to Hurricane Fly in 2011. **Thousand Stars** hasn't failed by much in the last 2 runnings of this race, a neck behind Oscar Whisky on both occasions, at his very best here and needing no excuses, giving all he could on the flat but never quite getting there; he's extremely tough and will presumably head to Punchestown again next month, having finished second there after this race last year. **Rock On Ruby** was fresh when winning the Champion Hurdle and must have taken plenty out of himself that day, weakening from the last here as if still feeling those exertions; this trip isn't a problem for him, despite his rapid progress this season having come at 2m. **Third Intention** did as well as could be expected faced with a stiff task, feeling the pinch from the turn in. **Zarkandar** is worth sticking with at this trip and further but there is a suspicion that he's just a bit lazy rather than necessarily a stayer, already pushed along here when crashing out at the sixth, too far out to know how he'd have fared.

TIMEFORM'S BEST OF 2011/12

History doesn't always feel like history when you are living through it. There was, however, no mistaking a sense of racing history in the 2011/12 jumps season, which provided more than its share of "were you watching?" moments. Indeed, it is difficult to single out a specific highlight, be it Kauto Star rolling back the years to claim a record-breaking fifth win in the King George VI Chase or Big Buck's breaking the long-standing unbeaten record over jumps (previously held by triple champion hurdler Sir Ken). In addition, there were the breathtaking displays by outstanding novice chaser Sprinter Sacre, yet another jockeys' championship for the remarkable Tony McCoy (he's now won seventeen in a row!) and the closest-ever finish in Grand National history. As a result, 2012/13 has plenty to live up to!

Staying Chasers

Kauto Star defeating Long Run to gain a record-breaking fifth win in the King George

Kauto Star (c179) defied his years to reverse 2010/11 form with much-younger rival **Long Run** (c178) when claiming emotional wins in both the Betfair Chase at Haydock and the King George at Kempton, performances which cemented his position as the greatest chaser since Arkle's era. Although admittedly not quite the force of old (he was c191 at his very peak), Kauto Star still finished the campaign as Timeform's top-rated chaser for the fifth time in six seasons. Long Run remains a force to be reckoned with despite those reverses to Kauto Star, plus his below-par third to the ill-fated **Synchronised** (c167) in the Cheltenham Gold Cup, and it should be remembered that a reproduction of his sole 2011/12 victory (in the Betfair Denman Chase at Newbury) would have been good enough to defend his Gold Cup crown successfully—surprise Cheltenham runner-up **The Giant Bolster** (165), for example, was a well-held fourth in the Newbury race. The Irish challenge in this division was again rather a weak one, particularly after one-time Gold Cup hopeful **Quito de La Roque** (c161) was ruled out for much of the campaign due to a sinus problem. Irish Hennessy winner **Quel Esprit** (c161) briefly looked like making the grade, but he had his limitations exposed somewhat when managing only third behind the exposed pair **China Rock** (c164) and **Follow The Plan** (c163) at Punchestown on his final start.

Two-mile Chasers

By contrast, Irish-trained chasers can boast a very strong record over the minimum trip in recent years, though even that looked to be on the wane in 2011/12. **Big Zeb** (c164d) shaped very much as if old age is catching up with him during the second half of the campaign, whilst multiple Grade 1 winner **Golden Silver** (c149) fell fatally at Leopardstown in December. **Sizing Europe** (c172) showed himself to be every bit as good as ever with four wins, notably an impressive display in the Tingle Creek at Sandown, but even he had to settle for second place behind **Finian's Rainbow** (c174) when defending his crown in the Queen Mother Champion Chase at Cheltenham. The good news for connections of Sizing Europe is that they probably won't have deal with Finian's Rainbow at around two miles again in 2012/13—that gelding is due to tackle longer trips this winter, with his impressive win over two and a half miles at Aintree in April suggesting he could join stable-companion **Riverside Theatre** (c170) as a live contender for the Ryanair Chase come next year's Cheltenham Festival. The bad news, of course, is that they'll have to contend with Sprinter Sacre instead!

Novice Chasers

A sparkling unbeaten campaign earned **Sprinter Sacre** (c175p) the highest Timeform rating ever awarded to a novice chaser since our Chasers & Hurdlers series began in 1975/6, whilst it also meant he ended the season as our top-rated two-mile chaser. Indeed, it proved to be a vintage season in the novice chasing ranks. The talented but quirky **Sanctuaire** (c169) was a revelation once switched to fences midway through the campaign and it would be unwise to underestimate the third of his wide-margin wins (in the Celebration Chase at Sandown) solely on the grounds that several of his rivals were over the top by that stage of the season. In addition to Sanctuaire, the Nicholls stable housed two other novices who acquitted themselves very well in open company at around the minimum trip, namely **Al Ferof** (c158) and **Edgardo Sol** (c160). The latter showed dramatic improvement during 2011/12, though his rate of progress paled into insignificance when compared to that of the remarkable **Hunt Ball** (c160), whose Cheltenham Festival win was his seventh of the campaign, whilst he also held his own in Grade 1 company when third in the Aintree Bowl on his final outing. **Bobs Worth** (c159p) and **Silviniaco Conti** (c158) were kept solely to novice company and looked top-class prospects when winning at Cheltenham and Aintree respectively, whilst it's too soon to be writing off their Kempton conqueror **Grands Crus** (c157p) despite his flop in the RSA Chase. The most interesting staying novice chaser of 2011/12, however, was the unbeaten **Sir des Champs** (c164p), who already looks to have strong claims of emulating his owner's War of Attrition by winning the Cheltenham Gold Cup. Come next March, the Irish could well another live Gold Cup contender in

Flemenstar (c163), who ran up an impressive sequence on home soil during the second half of 2011/12 and promises to be equally as effective when stepped up to three miles.

Staying Hurdlers

Timeform's top staying hurdler has been rated higher than its two-mile counterpart in nine of the last eleven seasons and there is little sign of that domination ending so long as **Big Buck's** (h176+) continues to exert his vice-like grip on the staying division. It was a record-breaking campaign in more ways than one for Big Buck's, who looked every bit as good as ever when claiming his fourth straight win in the World Hurdle, beating a strong field that included the non-staying pair **Oscar Whisky** (h167) and **Thousand Stars** (h163)—that duo franked the form by going on to fight out a close finish to the Aintree Hurdle for the second year running. Oscar Whisky will presumably drop back to around two miles if kept over hurdles in 2012/13, though the fact Thousand Stars has now won the French Champion Hurdle twice suggests he's well worth another try at the World Hurdle trip. **Voler La Vedette** (h159) ended up giving Big Buck's most to do at Cheltenham, though it is another Irish-trained mare who appeals as the only serious rival to him, namely **Quevega** (h164). Alas, the pair haven't come close to meeting yet, largely due to Quevega's connections understandably plumping for the easy pickings on offer elsewhere at the Cheltenham Festival in the David Nicholson Mares' Hurdle—a race she also won for the fourth year running in 2011/12. Given that Ruby Walsh is the regular pilot on both horses, he'll presumably be keen they continue to be kept apart!

Big Bucks (right) on his way to landing a fourth World Hurdle

Two-mile Hurdlers

Walsh can often be the victim of his own success, as was the case in the latest Champion Hurdle, when he missed the winning ride on **Rock On Ruby** (h171). Due to his role as stable jockey to both Paul Nicholls and Willie Mullins, Walsh had to choose between six possible mounts (in a field of just ten!) for the latest Champion, with Rock On Ruby third choice in the betting amongst that sextet. Walsh remained loyal to 2011 winner **Hurricane Fly** (h173) and, although he could manage only a below-par third in the 2012 renewal, time is likely to show that he remains the better horse. Indeed, Hurricane Fly had looked better than ever when winning the Irish Champion Hurdle on his Cheltenham prep run, whilst a workmanlike win under very testing conditions at Punchestown in April took his record over hurdles to thirteen wins from sixteen starts (placed in Grade 1 company on the other three), so he'll clearly be a force to be reckoned with for a good while longer yet. Nicky Henderson holds a strong hand in the two-mile hurdling division, even though he had to rely solely on 2010 winner **Binocular** (h164) come the Champion itself, that gelding's fourth place there a bit below the form of his wins in the Christmas Hurdle (when beating Rock On Ruby) and Kingwell Hurdle. Stable-companion **Grandouet** (h164) was forced to miss the race through injury, though the form of his International Hurdle win was boosted by runner-up **Overturn** (h165) going on to fill that same position in the Champion.

Novice Hurdlers (inc Juveniles)

Henderson could have a couple more Champion Hurdle contenders on his hands in **Simonsig** (h162p) and **Darlan** (h152p). As their respective ratings would imply, Simonsig appeals as the better prospect—indeed, he is one of the most exciting prospects to come through the novice hurdling ranks in recent seasons and the sky is the limit for him, regardless of whether connections opt for the chasing or hurdling route in 2012/13. Darlan couldn't quite match Simonsig's Cheltenham-Aintree double, though he was arguably unlucky when runner-up to **Cinders And Ashes** (h149p) in the Supreme at the former track, whilst his smooth display when winning the Top Novices' at Aintree suggests he'll be able to hold his own in good two-mile company over the coming months. The top staying novices weren't too shabby either! **Fingal Bay** (h156p) inflicted the only defeat on Simonsig when outstaying him at Sandown in December and remains a top-notch prospect despite having to settle for second behind **Lovcen** (h149) at Aintree on his final start (a late setback forced him to miss the Cheltenham Festival). Similar comments apply to Ireland's top novice hurdler **Boston Bob** (h154p), even though he failed to justify short-priced favouritism when runner-up to the ill-fated **Brindisi Breeze** (h150) in the Spa Hurdle at Cheltenham. Boston Bob arguably wasn't seen to best advantage in the Spa, whilst it's worth stressing that the form of his two previous wins in Ireland proved to be very strong. The leading juveniles were a likeable, but far from vintage, bunch. That phrase certainly sums up surprise Triumph winner **Countrywide Flame** (h147), who showed admirable battling qualities (plus stamina reserves) in the Triumph but had to settle for minor honours in Grade 1 company either side of that Cheltenham win, including when runner-up to Triumph third **Grumeti** (h148) at Aintree on his final start.

2011/12 STATISTICS

TRAINERS (1,2,3 earnings)	Horses	Indiv'l Wnrs	Races Won	Runs	Strike Rate	Stakes £
1 Paul Nicholls	182	86	138	598	23.0	3,141,353
2 Nicky Henderson	193	100	167	627	26.6	2,597,194
3 Donald McCain	168	90	153	717	21.3	1,186,499
4 Jonjo O'Neill	157	63	97	649	14.9	1,101,362
5 Alan King	142	55	82	523	15.6	1,066,393
6 David Pipe	156	69	101	632	15.9	898,427
7 Philip Hobbs	142	46	73	512	14.2	801,936
8 Nigel Twiston-Davies	135	42	70	579	12.0	601,559
9 Tim Vaughan	174	67	102	592	17.2	520,000
10 Evan Williams	136	55	88	579	15.1	496,333

JOCKEYS (by winners)	1st	2nd	3rd	Unpl	Total Rides	Strike Rate
1 A P McCoy	199	128	77	322	726	27.4
2 Richard Johnson	153	152	115	414	834	18.3
3 Jason Maguire	144	115	68	297	624	23.0
4 Daryl Jacob	83	77	48	247	455	18.2
5 Tom O'Brien	83	57	51	345	536	15.4
6 Paddy Brennan	82	74	53	267	476	17.2
7 Sam Twiston-Davies	81	91	68	358	598	13.5
8 Paul Moloney	70	65	56	356	547	12.7
9 Tom Scudamore	65	53	53	278	449	14.4
10 Barry Geraghty	63	37	17	103	220	28.6

SIRES OF WINNERS (1,2,3 earnings)	Races Won	Runs	Strike Rate	Stakes £
1 King's Theatre (by Sadler's Wells)	69	429	16.0	949,903
2 Oscar (by Sadler's Wells)	79	566	13.9	882,220
3 Dom Alco (by Dom Pasquini)	15	85	17.6	827,283
4 Old Vic (by Sadler's Wells)	84	514	16.3	702,402
5 Cadoudal (by Green Dancer)	12	66	18.1	582,124
6 Accordion (by Sadler's Wells)	36	230	15.6	543,340
7 Milan (by Sadler's Wells)	86	458	18.7	537,273
8 Flemensfirth (by Alleged)	88	532	16.5	533,597
9 Sadler's Wells (by Northern Dancer)	36	242	14.8	501,702
10 Beneficial (by Top Ville)	87	615	14.1	500,767

LEADING HORSES (1,2,3 earnings)	Races Won	Runs	Stakes £
1 Neptune Collonges 11 gr.g Dom Alco–Castille Collonges	1	5	572,536
2 Finian's Rainbow 9 b.g Tiraaz–Trinity Gale	3	4	328,685
3 Synchronised 9 b.g Sadler's Wells–Mayasta	1	4	292,775
4 Big Buck's 9 b.g Cadoudal–Buck's	5	5	292,649
5 Rock On Ruby 7 b.g Oscar–Stony View	2	4	254,036
6 Overturn 8 b.g Barathea–Kristal Bridge	3	6	248,148
7 Sunnyhillboy 9 b.g Old Vic–Sizzle	1	5	235,803
8 Riverside Theatre 8 b.g King's Theatre–Disallowed	2	3	232,548
9 Kauto Star 12 b.g Village Star–Kauto Relka	2	3	216,064
10 Sprinter Sacre 6 b.g Network–Fatima III	5	5	164,160

SECTION 5

THE TIMEFORM TOP 100

HURDLERS

Rating	Horse
176+	Big Buck's
173	Hurricane Fly
171	Rock On Ruby
167	Oscar Whisky
165	Overturn
164	Binocular
164	Grandouet
164	Quevega
163	Thousand Stars
162p	Simonsig
162	Celestial Halo
161	Zarkandar
160	Get Me Out of Here
160	Oscars Well
160	Zaidpour
159	Smad Place
159	Voler La Vedette
158	Any Given Day
158	Brampour
158	Dynaste
157	Cape Tribulation
157	Eradicate
157	Mourad
156p	Fingal Bay
156§	Tidal Bay
156	So Young
155	The Real Article
154p	Boston Bob
154§	Zaynar
154	Attaglance
154	Mikael d'Haguenet
153+	Unaccompanied
152p	Darlan
152	Carlito Brigante
152	Featherbed Lane
152	Pittoni
152	Poungach
152	Snap Tie
151+	Grands Crus
151	Blackstairmountain
151	Shot From The Hip
150	Brindisi Breeze
150	Cousin Vinny
150	Luska Lad
150	Menorah
150	Staying Article
149p	Cinders And Ashes
149	Felix Yonger
149	Final Approach
149	Lovcen
149	Whatuthink
148	Gibb River
148	King of The Night
148	Raya Star
148	Restless Harry
148	Sailors Warn
147p	Dedigout
147p	Montbazon
147	Captain Cee Bee
147	Clerk's Choice
147	Donnas Palm
147	Grand Vision
147	Jack Cool
147	Moon Dice
147	Sire de Grugy
147	Sweet My Lord
147	Synchronised
147	Third Intention
147	Tofino Bay
147	Trifolium
146§	Sanctuaire
146	Alderwood
146	Catch Me
146	Cotton Mill
146	Powerstation
146	Prospect Wells
146	Saphir River
145	Ambion Wood
145	Colour Squadron
145	Fosters Cross
145	Lifestyle
145	Marsh Warbler
145	Mossey Joe
145	Oscar Dan Dan
145	Pettifour
145	The Knoxs
144	Benash
144	Benny Be Good
144	Cantlow
144	Fully Funded
144	Jumbo Rio
144	Lyreen Legend
144	Mount Benbulben
144	Oneeightofamile
144	Petit Robin
144	Sergent Guib's
143	Askanna
143	Barker
143	Cross Kennon
143	Dare To Doubt
143	Dirar
143	Dream Esteem
143	Five Dream
143	General Miller
143	Houblon des Obeaux
143	Ipsos du Berlais
143	Mad Moose
143	Son of Flicka
143	Spirit River
143	Twinlight
143	Via Galilei

CHASERS

Rating	Horse
179	Kauto Star
178	Long Run
175p	Sprinter Sacre
174	Finian's Rainbow
172	Master Minded
172	Sizing Europe
170	Riverside Theatre
169	Sanctuaire
168	Poquelin
167	Albertas Run
167	Medermit
167	Synchronised
166	Neptune Collonges
165§	Tidal Bay
165	Captain Chris
165	Realt Dubh
165	Somersby
165	The Giant Bolster
164p	Sir des Champs
164	Big Zeb
164	China Rock
164	Weird Al
163+	Flemenstar
163	Follow The Plan
163	Tataniano
162	Burton Port
162	Great Endeavour
162	Midnight Chase
162	Rubi Light
162	Wishfull Thinking
161	Kauto Stone
161	Nacarat
161	Quel Esprit
161	Quito de La Roque
160	Calgary Bay
160	Cue Card
160	Edgardo Sol
160	Hunt Ball
159p	Bobs Worth
159	Gauvain
159	Hey Big Spender
159	Junior
159	Menorah
158§	What A Friend

158	Al Ferof
158	Joncol
158	Noble Prince
158	Silviniaco Conti
158	Time For Rupert
157p	Grands Crus
157	First Lieutenant
157	I'msingingtheblues
157	Planet of Sound
157	Tanks For That
157	Tranquil Sea
157	Woolcombe Folly
156p	The Minack
156	Ballabriggs
156	Diamond Harry
156	French Opera
156	Mon Parrain
156	Quantitativeeasing
155	Benny Be Good
155	Champion Court
155	Master of The Hall
155	Prince de Beauchene
155	Roudoudou Ville
154	Captain Cee Bee
154	Cornas
154	Roberto Goldback
154	Scotsirish
154	Seabass
154	The Nightingale
153	Chicago Grey
153	Forpadydeplasterer
153	Lucky William
153	Rebel du Maquis
152	Aerial
152	Bog Warrior
152	Cappa Bleu
152	For Non Stop
152	Ghizao
152	Oiseau de Nuit
152	Tchico Polos
152	West With The Wind
151§	Tamarinbleu
151	Auroras Encore
151	Blackstairmountain
151	Blazing Tempo
151	Cristal Bonus
151	Massini's Maguire
151	Sunnyhillboy
150+	Salut Flo
150	Alfa Beat
150	Apt Approach
150	Deep Purple
150	Mossey Joe
150	Rathlin
150	Roi du Mee
150	Shakalakaboomboom
150	Tartak

JUVENILE HURDLERS

148	Grumeti
147	Countrywide Flame
144	Sadler's Risk
143	Hisaabaat
142	Baby Mix
142	Pearl Swan
141p	Balder Succes
141p	Dodging Bullets
140p	Ranjaan
140	Ut de Sivola
140	Vendor
139	Edeymi
139	Kazlian
138	Lexi's Boy
138	Shadow Catcher
137	Hinterland
137	Hollow Tree
137	Urbain de Sivola
137	Wingtips
136	Taruma

NOVICE HURDLERS

162p	Simonsig
156p	Fingal Bay
154p	Boston Bob
152p	Darlan
150	Brindisi Breeze
149p	Cinders And Ashes
149	Felix Yonger
149	Lovcen
147p	Dedigout
147p	Montbazon
147	Grand Vision
147	Trifolium
146	Alderwood
146	Cotton Mill
146	Prospect Wells
145	Ambion Wood
145	Colour Squadron
144	Lyreen Legend
144	Mount Benbulben
143	Ipsos du Berlais

NOVICE CHASERS

175p	Sprinter Sacre
169	Sanctuaire
164p	Sir des Champs
163+	Flemenstar
160	Cue Card
160	Edgardo Sol
160	Hunt Ball
159p	Bobs Worth
159	Menorah
158	Al Ferof
158	Silviniaco Conti
157p	Grands Crus
157	First Lieutenant
155	Champion Court
153	Lucky William
152	Bog Warrior
152	For Non Stop
151	Blackstairmountain
151	Cristal Bonus
150	Mossey Joe
150	Rathlin

NATIONAL HUNT FLAT HORSES

128	Don Cossack
127	Champagne Fever
125	Pique Sous
124	Buckers Bridge
123	New Year's Eve
121	Simonsig
121	The New One
120	My Tent Or Yours
119	Moscow Mannon
118p	Lord of Lords
118	Clonbanan Lad
118	Melodic Rendezvous
118	Rory O'Moore
118	Sir Johnson
118	Up To Something
118	Yes Way Hosay
117p	Un Atout
117	Mozoltov
116	Thomas Edison
115	Atlanta Falcon
115	Hazy Tom
115	Royal Guardsman

HUNTER CHASERS

147	Takeroc*
139	Salsify
139	Vic Venturi*
138	Chapoturgeon
138	Gwanako
135	I Have Dreamed
134	Monkerty Tunkerty
134	Saddlers Storm*
134	That's Rhythm
133+	Marky Bob
133	Bradley*
133	Earth Dream
132	Hoo La Baloo*
132	Postmaster*
130	Barbers Shop
128x	Turko
128	Blackstaff
128	Oscar Delta

* = Highest rating achieved in a non-hunter

PROMISING HORSES

A p symbol is used by Timeform to denote horses we believe are capable of improvement, with a P symbol suggesting a horse is capable of much better form. Below is a list of selected British- and Irish-trained horses with a p or P, listed under their current trainers.

Horse	Age/Sex	Rating	Rating
WILLIAM AMOS			
Lie Forrit (IRE)	8 b.g	h150	c133p
JIM BEST			
Western High	7 b.g	h95p	
HENRY DE BROMHEAD, IRELAND			
Days Hotel (IRE)	7 b.g	h127	c140p
CHARLES BYRNES, IRELAND			
Knockfierna (IRE)	7 b.m		c146p
REBECCA CURTIS			
At Fishers Cross (IRE)	5 b.g	h110p	F110
VICTOR DARTNALL			
Sleeping City (FR)	5 b.g	h118p	
ROBIN DICKIN			
Restless Harry	8 b.g	h148	c142p
TIM EASTERBY			
Crackentorp	7 b.g	h116p	
King of The Celts (IRE)	4 b.g	h102p	
BRIAN ELLISON			
Hada Men (USA)	7 b.g	h129p	
RICHARD FAHEY			
High Office	6 b.g	h95p	
Mica Mika (IRE)	4 ch.g	h106p	
TOM GEORGE			
Forgotten Gold (IRE)	6 b.g	h129p	
Module (FR)	5 b.g	h135p	
Nodebateaboutit	7 b.g	h89p	c117p
Rody (FR)	7 ch.g	h99	c118p
JIM GOLDIE			
Merchant of Dubai	7 b.g	h103p	
WARREN GREATREX			
Paint The Clouds	7 b.g	h126+	c128p
Private Eyes (IRE)	6 b.g	F101p	
NICKY HENDERSON			
Bobs Worth (IRE)	7 b.g		c159p
Broadbackbob (IRE)	7 b.g	h139p	
Cape Express (IRE)	7 b.g	h129p	
Chatterbox (IRE)	4 b.g	F102p	
Darlan	5 br.g	h152p	
Featherintheattic (IRE)	7 b.g	h122p	
Fourth Estate (IRE)	6 b.g	h124p	
Foxbridge (IRE)	6 b.g	h112p	
Hadrian's Approach (IRE)	5 b.g	h136p	
Keys (IRE)	5 b.g	h129p	
Malt Master (IRE)	5 b.g	h132p	
Master of The Game (IRE)	6 ch.g	h125p	
Mono Man (IRE)	6 b.g	h132p	
Oscara Dara (IRE)	7 b.g	h139p	
Simonsig	6 gr.g	h162p	
Snake Eyes (IRE)	4 b.g	F105p	
Sprinter Sacre (FR)	6 b.g	h152p	c175p
PHILIP HOBBS			
Arthurian Legend	7 b.g	h134	c—p
Fingal Bay (IRE)	6 b.g	h156p	
Itsalark (IRE)	6 b.m	F102p	
Jayandbee (IRE)	5 b.g	h97p	
Princely Player (IRE)	5 b.g	h129p	
ANTHONY HONEYBALL			
Fountains Flypast	8 b.g	h130p	
Regal Encore (IRE)	4 b.g	F84p	
Royal Announcement	5 b.g	F77p	
Swincombe Stone	5 ch.g	F92p	
Velator	5 b.g	h125p	
Victors Serenade (IRE)	7 b.g	h122+	c143p
ALAN KING			
Balder Succes (FR)	4 b.g	h141p	
Batonnier (FR)	6 ch.g	h135p	
Diamond Sweeper (IRE)	6 b.g	h110p	
Invictus (IRE)	6 b.g		c148p
Montbazon (FR)	5 b.g	h147p	
No Substitute (IRE)	7 b.g	h118p	
Woodyoulikeme	4 ch.g	F102p	
EMMA LAVELLE			
Blues And Twos	6 b.g	h108p	c133p
Captain Sunshine	6 b.g	h139p	
Claret Cloak (IRE)	5 b.g	h127p	
Elegant Touch (IRE)	6 b.m	h122p	
Grey Wulff (IRE)	7 gr.g		c126p
Kentford Grey Lady	6 gr.m	h136p	
Kindly Note	5 ch.m	h111p	
Penny Max (IRE)	6 b.g		c140p
The Last Night (FR)	5 ch.g	h102p	
CHARLIE LONGSDON			
Brassick	5 b.g	F104p	
Hayjack	7 b.g	h121p	
No No Bingo (IRE)	6 b.g	h102p	
Pendra (IRE)	4 ch.g	F105p	

Ravastree (IRE) 6 b.g c116p
Spirit of Shankly 4 ch.g F102p

A. J. MARTIN, IRELAND

Dedigout (IRE) 6 b.g h147p

DONALD MCCAIN

Bound For Glory (IRE) 6 b.g h112p
Cinders And Ashes 5 b.g h149p
Diocles (IRE) 6 b.g h123p
King's Grace 6 b.g h118p
Real Milan (IRE) 7 b.g h136p
Tarlan (IRE) 6 b.g h112p
Ubaltique (FR) 4 b.g h129p

NOEL MEADE, IRELAND

Ange Blanc (FR) 4 gr.g F100p
Corbally Ghost (IRE) 5 gr.g h125p F111
Sword of Destiny (IRE) 6 gr.g h131P

GARY MOORE

Grabtheglory (IRE) 6 b.g h121p

W. P. MULLINS, IRELAND

Aupcharlie (IRE) 6 b.g h133p
Boston Bob (IRE) 7 b.g h154p
Marito (GER) 6 b.g h142p
Sir des Champs (FR) 6 b.g h146p c164p
Soll 7 ch.g h114p c134p
The Bosses Cousin (IRE) 7 b.g h115p
Un Atout (FR) 4 br.g F117p
Up The Beat 7 b.g c144p

PAUL NICHOLLS

Black Thunder (FR) 5 bl.g h138p
Bold Addition (FR) 7 b.g h129 c124p
Bold Chief (IRE) 7 br.g h132p
Broomfield 5 b.g h118p
Dodging Bullets 4 b.g h141p
Escudero (IRE) 7 ch.g h116p
Final Gift (IRE) 6 b.g h105p
Italian Master (IRE) 6 b.g h107p
Merehead (FR) 6 gr.g h123p
Promising Anshan (IRE) 7 ch.g h121p c136
Rangitoto (IRE) 7 b.g h125p c135p
Ranjaan (FR) 4 b.g h140p
Rolling Aces (IRE) 6 b.g h121p
Salubrious (IRE) 5 b.g h125p F110
Sam Winner (FR) 5 b.g h146 c123p
The Minack (IRE) 8 b.g c156p
Watergate Bay (IRE) 6 b.g h121p

JONJO O'NEILL

Cross The Flags (IRE) 5 b.m h128p
Master Milan (IRE) 6 b.g h106p c119
Tigresse Bleue 4 b.f h103p
Washington Road (IRE) 5 b.g h117p
Well Hello There (IRE) 6 b.g h131p
Wild Rhubarb 7 ch.m h116p

DAVID PIPE

Arrayan 7 b.g c118p
Buddy Bolero (IRE) 6 b.g h122p
Bygones Sovereign (IRE) 6 b.g h117p
Grands Crus (FR) 7 gr.g h151+ c157p
Laflammedeglorie 6 b.g h100p
Problema Tic (FR) 6 b.g h128+ c143p
Swing Bowler 5 b.m h120p
Top Wood (FR) 5 ch.g h119p
War Singer (USA) 5 b.g h107p
Wings of Icarus (IRE) 5 ch.g h105p

JOHN QUINN

Moonlight Drive (IRE) 6 b.g h125 c121p

KEITH REVELEY

Harvey's Hope 6 b.g h115p
Seren Gris 6 gr.m h111p
Special Catch (IRE) 5 b.g h116p F100

NICKY RICHARDS

Abbey Garth (IRE) 5 b.g h104p F95
Next To Nowhere (IRE) 7 ch.g h96p c99p
One For Hocky (IRE) 4 b.g F95p

PAULINE ROBSON

Rival d'Estruval (FR) 7 b.g h129 c129p

C. ROCHE, IRELAND

Ballynacree (IRE) 4 b.g h131p

LUCINDA RUSSELL

Bold Sir Brian (IRE) 6 b.g c143p
Nuts N Bolts 6 b.g h122p
Tap Night (USA) 5 ch.g h140p

ALAN SWINBANK

George Adamson (IRE) 6 b.g h111p
Gogeo (IRE) 5 b.g h106p

MARTIN TODHUNTER

See What Happens (IRE) 6 b.g h116p

ANDY TURNELL

Gotoyourplay (IRE) 8 ch.g c127p

TIM VAUGHAN

Explained (IRE) 5 b.g F106p

EVAN WILLIAMS

Alla Svelta (IRE) 6 b.g h126p
Barrakilla (IRE) 5 b.g F93p
Gurtacrue (IRE) 7 ch.g c123p
Oscar Sunset (IRE) 5 b.g h129p F90
Prima Porta 6 b.m h109p
Zarzal (IRE) 4 b.g h117p

NICK WILLIAMS

Kateal 9 b.m h119+ c127p
Ulis de Vassy (FR) 4 b.g h115p

VENETIA WILLIAMS

Definite Memories (IRE) 5 b.m h113p
Reginaldinho (UAE) 6 b.g h102 c109p

COURSE POINTERS

The following A-Z guide covers all racecourses in England, Scotland and Wales that stage racing over jumps. An overview is provided of each course's characteristics, along with in-running pointers.

AINTREE

➤ The Mildmay Course is flat with sharp bends and, when the going is good or firmer, it is very much a course which favours speedy types. Conversely, when the going is testing the nature of the track changes completely, stamina very much at a premium on soft/heavy, well-run races under testing conditions often resulting in few finishers.

➤ The National Course covers two and a quarter miles and is perfectly flat throughout, and the ground is often slightly more testing than on the Mildmay Course. Despite most races being well run, there is a definite advantage with those who race prominently, especially in races short of the Grand National distance.

ASCOT

➤ Right handed, galloping.

➤ NH course reopened in 2006/7 after major redevelopment work, and improved drainage means conditions rarely get so testing as they used to.

➤ Fences used to be amongst the stiffest in the country but recent evidence suggests this is no longer the case, with just 24 fallers from 610 runners over fences from the 2006/7-2011/12 seasons.

➤ The chase course has tended to favour those ridden prominently since the redevelopment.

AYR

➤ Left handed.

➤ A course whose character changes dramatically on account of the going; it's one of the most gruelling in the country on heavy ground, yet conversely becomes a sharp test when the going is firm.

➤ The fences are fairly stiff and account for more than their share of casualties, though this is probably partly due to the fact that so many meetings take place on very testing ground. The first in the home straight catches out plenty, possibly on account of it coming so soon after the turn.

➤ No particular type of tactics are especially rewarding, though as usual being held up under firmish conditions has its pitfalls.

BANGOR-ON-DEE

➤ Left handed, fairly sharp.

➤ Races invariably well run, possibly on account of runners being on the turn pretty much throughout, though this doesn't prevent front runners being advantaged on the hurdles course.

➤ Fences generally regarded as being fairly stiff for a lesser NH course, though recent evidence doesn't support this.

➤ Last two fences arguably the trickiest on the course.

CARLISLE

➤ Right handed, undulating, most galloping.

➤ A notably stiff track on account of the home straight being uphill, though as a consequence many races are steadily run with riders keen to conserve the energy of their mounts.

➤ A new hurdles course was constructed on the inside of the chase track prior to the 2011/12 season and is appreciably tighter than the old one. The old one (situated on the Flat course) will be used very sparingly in the future.

➤ Fences are statistically the easiest in the country (only 2.7% fallers 2005/6-2011/12).

➤ Invariably extremely testing ground in mid-winter.

CARTMEL

➤ Left handed, tight.

➤ Only six fences to a circuit places little emphasis on jumping, though they are fairly stiff for a minor course and result in a disproportionate number of unseats to falls.

➤ Run-in of half a mile from the last fence is longest in the country and, unsurprisingly, the lead changes hands from the last more than would normally be expected.

CATTERICK BRIDGE

➤ Left handed, sharp with minor undulations.

➤ Fences generally regarded as fairly easy, but chases are invariably well run and result in many more casualties than might be expected.

➤ Going rarely gets that testing, with nippy sorts generally at an advantage over gallopers who take time to quicken.

➤ Beware deceptive camera angle as runners swing into the home straight, those who stay towards the centre often seeming closer to the lead than they actually are.

CHELTENHAM

➤ Left handed, undulating.

➤ Improved drainage has resulted in the going rarely being so testing as used to be the case.

➤ Stiff fences, though the notoriously tricky downhill one before the home turn has now been moved into the straight on safety grounds.

➤ Last half mile is uphill, although the lead changes hands on the run-in less frequently than might be expected, whilst last-fence/flight casualties are rare.

➤ Horses who race prominently often fare well on the chase course, especially in races up to 2m4f100yds.

➤ Hurdles track on the New Course has just two flights in the last six furlongs, resulting in less emphasis on jumping and more on stamina in many races; large-field races over two miles often go to horses who've come from well off the pace, as there can be a tendency to go for home plenty soon enough.

➤ Cross-country course has a wide range of obstacles, the vast majority of which place little emphasis on jumping ability; races tend to be run at a pedestrian pace thanks to the extremely tight nature of the track. Previous cross-country experience has proved to be of benefit, including so far as riders are concerned as well as horses.

CHEPSTOW

➤ Left handed, undulating.

➤ Front runners historically do well over fences, almost certainly on account of there being five obstacles in the home straight, the first part of which is downhill. This holds good whether underfoot conditions place the emphasis on speed or stamina.

➤ Chase course no more than averagely tricky to negotiate, with the downhill fences in the home straight catching out more than the six on the other side of the course.

DONCASTER

➤ Left handed, galloping and essentially flat.

➤ Extremely well-draining course, conditions often favouring speedier types despite its galloping nature.

EXETER

➤ Right handed, hilly, galloping, with the chase track situated on the outside of the hurdles one.

➤ Conditions can get exceptionally testing in mid-winter and the exact opposite in drier periods, the course being without an artificial watering system.

➤ By and large, races over both hurdles and fences tend to be steadily run, with the long downhill run before the first obstacle in the back straight encouraging riders to take things steady and prepare for the uphill climb.

➤ The chase course is no more than averagely difficult to negotiate, with plenty of trainers viewing it as the ideal course to introduce chasing debutants.

➤ Be wary of the course executive switching the hurdlers on to the chase track whenever it suits.

FAKENHAM

➤ Left handed, very sharp.

➤ The tightest track in the country and, in theory, ideal for handy, front-running types as opposed to long-striding gallopers, though underfoot conditions are often more testing than advertised and races are invariably strongly-run, too, resulting in the emphasis being much more on stamina than might be expected.

➤ As a result, there are a high proportion of casualties over fences for a minor track, well above the UK average in recent years.

FFOS LAS

➤ A wide, galloping, left-handed circuit of 1½ miles, with a straight of just over 4f.

➤ It has no undulations but a very slight rise over the course of the back straight and the opposite in the home straight.

➤ The ground can become extremely testing in the winter, placing an emphasis on stamina.

➤ Fallers/unseats are largely in line with the UK average.

➤ There are short run-ins for both hurdles and chases.

FOLKESTONE

➤ Right handed, undulating.

➤ The fences are extremely easy—from 2004/5-2011/12 there were only 89 fallers/unseats from a total of 1757 runners.

➤ The ground on the hurdles course (which is also used on the Flat and is therefore watered during the summer) can get extremely testing, with conditions on the chase track favouring speedier types on the whole.

FONTWELL PARK

➤ Left handed; the chase course is a tight figure of eight circuit, whilst the hurdles track is oval and also essentially sharp in nature, but with a stiff finish which can make for a thorough test of stamina on testing ground.

➤ The fences are relatively easy but, unsurprisingly given the nature of the chase track, course specialists do abound.

➤ On the chase course, the horse in front often displays a tendency to idle on the run-in before picking up again when challenged, meaning the lead rarely changes hands but often looks as though it might.

➤ On the hurdles course, be aware that the paddock exit is situated halfway up the run-in and can lead to horses idling/ducking out on seeing it, especially if they're in front and have nothing else in their eye-line.

HAYDOCK

➤ Left handed, flat.

➤ Conditions often extremely testing during mid-winter, with an ability to cope with gruelling conditions being of paramount importance. Conversely, conditions at the Swinton Meeting in May usually place the emphasis very much on speed, with a tendency to favour those ridden prominently as a result.

➤ Recently redeveloped NH track, now situated inside the flat courses with both hurdles and chases (portable fences) taking place on the same strip of ground.

➤ Formerly held an undeserved reputation as one of the hardest courses in the country to jump round, something which most certainly isn't backed up by statistics, but recent evidence suggests the new portable fences provide little in the way of a jumping test.

HEREFORD

➤ Right handed.

➤ A course whose character alters dramatically depending on the state of the ground; it can present a gruelling test of stamina on heavy going but, conversely, is essentially a sharp track which favours speedier sorts when the ground is firmer than good.

➤ The fences are relatively easy, though chases here attract larger fields than most courses and can result in casualties simply through weight of numbers, especially in the lowest-grade races.

➤ Races have a tendency to be well run, though those run at a steadier pace can often change complexion very quickly on meeting rising ground towards the end of the back straight.

HEXHAM

➤ Left handed, undulating, with a steep climb from the end of the back straight to the finish.

➤ Races over hurdles generally steadily run, but be wary of horses kicked for home a long way out, the testing finish regularly catching out those who look to be moving comfortably in a clear lead before meeting the uphill section.

➤ Fences generally regarded as easy with few fallers, though there are a disproportionately high number of unseats.

HUNTINGDON

➤ Right handed, flat.

➤ Generally favours speedier types unless conditions are notably testing, with hold-up tactics over shorter distances (especially over hurdles) often hard to overcome.

➤ Fences claim a higher percentage of casualties than might be expected, possibly on account of many chases attracting largish fields and, especially under less testing conditions, being run at a decent pace.

KELSO

➤ Left handed, generally flat, with the hurdles course separate to the chase one and around a furlong shorter in length.

➤ On anything other than soft/heavy ground it's a track which is essentially sharp in character, especially over hurdles, and this will be probably be more so now that the formerly testing run-in has been shortened by around 200 yds during summer 2012, reducing the run from the last to just over a furlong.

➤ Chase course claims a higher than average number of fallers, with novices in particular finding it hard to negotiate.

KEMPTON PARK

➤ Right handed, flat.

➤ Can represent a much stiffer test of stamina than expected on soft/heavy going.

LEICESTER

➤ Right handed, rather undulating with a gradual uphill finish of around three furlongs.

➤ Hurdle races run on Flat course and usually more testing as a result, that track having been watered during the summer.

LINGFIELD PARK

➤ Left handed, undulating.

➤ Sharp in character on anything other than soft/heavy ground, a handy position into the straight often paying dividends, especially over fences.

➤ Fallers/unseats are below average for the UK.

➤ Bumper races usually run on the all-weather track nowadays; these are nearly always falsely-run affairs which count against stoutly-bred NH types.

LUDLOW

➤ Right handed, sharp.

➤ One of the best draining courses in the country, conditions rarely being worse than good to soft, and the emphasis nearly always very much on speed as a result.

➤ Well-run races more in evidence than at the majority of courses, though can be a tendency to overdo things in chases. Long run from the last in the back straight often leads to fields bunching up, an occurrence which is more frequent over hurdles.

➤ Fourth last used to be a notoriously tricky fence but was re-sited a few seasons back and catches fewer out nowadays, this possibly one of the reasons why the casualty rate since 2006/7 is lower than it used to be.

MARKET RASEN

➤ Right handed, sharp with minor undulations.

➤ Generally favours nippy types, plenty of races being won by those who quicken best on the run to the first obstacle in the home straight.

➤ Fairly easy fences, with the third last catching out fewer in recent seasons than used to be the case.

MUSSELBURGH

➤ Right handed, sharp, flat.

➤ Along with Ludlow one of the best draining NH courses in the country, conditions rarely worse than good to soft.

➤ Handy types typically seen to best advantage, with front runners/those who race prominently invariably faring well on the chase course.

➤ Higher than expected casualty rate over fences, possibly due to chases being both generally well run and attracting largely low-grade fields.

NEWBURY

➤ Left handed, galloping with few significant undulations.

➤ One of the fairest courses in the country, though it's galloping nature does make it ideal for the big, long-striding type.

➤ The chase course is generally regarded as being fairly stiff, though casualty figures have been about average in recent years, the fact that many races aren't run at a strong pace possibly contributes to these figures, as does the generally better standard of horse on show.

➤ Beware a sometimes deceptive camera angle early in the straight, runners often spread the width of the hurdles course yet their relative positions only coming clear at the third last.

➤ Leaders rarely overhauled on the chase run-in for all it often looks as though they might be, horses often displaying a tendency to idle from the last before picking up again once challenged, especially from the elbow.

NEWCASTLE

➤ Left handed, galloping with a steady uphill rise from the home turn.

➤ Stiff nature often results in steadily-run affairs, especially on the hurdles course, many races only really beginning in earnest once in line for home. As such, races often fail to represent the test of stamina they might.

➤ A position towards the stand rail can be an advantage in the home straight, and it's no coincidence that's where the senior northern jockeys usually head.

NEWTON ABBOT

➤ Left handed, tight.

➤ Favours handy types, with prominently-ridden horses at an advantage more often than not.

➤ Fences pose few problems.

➤ Very short run-in on hurdles course means the lead very rarely changes hands from the last.

PERTH

➤ Right handed, sharpish.

➤ Speedier types are generally favoured when the ground is good or firmer but conditions can get extremely testing on soft/heavy going.

➤ Fences not especially testing, with slightly lower than UK average fallers/unseats since 2004/5.

➤ The camera angle in the home straight is more or less head-on and, depending on the commentator's skill, marked fluctuations in in-running prices can occur unnecessarily.

PLUMPTON

➤ Left handed, tight and undulating.

➤ Despite the undulations, it's essentially a course which favours handy sorts thanks to the sharp turns.

➤ Races on the hurdles course often begin in earnest early on the final circuit, the complexion changing quickly at this point.

➤ Relatively high number of fallers, a figure which probably reflects the low standard of horses rather more than the stiffness of the fences.

➤ Beware those horses who stick to the inside on the hurdles track when the ground is testing, better going often found by racing wide.

SANDOWN PARK

➤ Right handed, galloping.

➤ Generally regarded as the one of the best jumping tests for chasers in the country, thanks chiefly to the seven fences in the back straight, the last three of which (the 'railway fences') are situated close together; however, the casualty rate isn't especially high, fallers in the home straight being very rare.

➤ Hurdles course often more testing than chase one during winter months, with gruelling conditions sometimes the order of the day on the former course.

➤ Front runners more favoured on the chase track, where it can regularly prove very hard to make up ground when conditions place the emphasis on speed.

SEDGEFIELD

➤ Left handed, undulating.

➤ In theory, uphill finish should dictate that plenty of races change complexion late in the day but, in practice, that isn't the case, the run-in on the hurdles course being short and plenty having a tendency to pick up again when challenged on the chase track.

SOUTHWELL

➤ Left handed, tight.

➤ Another course whose character changes dramatically depending on underfoot conditions, the emphasis being very much on speed on firmish ground yet completely the opposite on heavy ground, long-distance races under such conditions often resulting in very few finishers.

➤ The fences are of the portable variety and stiff for a minor track, a high number of casualties placing it in the top ten for fallers/unseats over the last five seasons.

➤ The brush-type hurdles penalise less fluent jumping more than the traditional variety.

STRATFORD

➤ Left handed, sharp.

➤ Has claimed a higher than average number of falls/unseats during recent seasons; the size of the fences obviously have something to do with this, but it's primarily down to the fact that so many races are well run, placing a greater emphasis on jumping.

➤ The hurdles track also has more than the normal number of well-run races, plenty of jockeys opting to strike for home sooner than they normally might because of the relatively short straight.

TAUNTON

➤ Right handed, sharp.

➤ Fences traditionally regarded as small and easy, yet surprisingly the casualty rate on the chase course is one of the highest in the country over the last eight seasons. The low quality of horses which contest the vast majority of races is undoubtedly an issue, whilst the sharp nature of the course is also a contributory factor.

TOWCESTER

➤ Right handed, extremely stiff.

➤ Final mile uphill and punishing in the extreme on testing ground, those horses who've gone freely and/or expended too much energy early invariably failing to get home. As such, be wary of taking short odds about horses who seem to be travelling strongly before the straight, as the complexion can often alter in a manner of strides.

➤ The fences aren't overly stiff, with the two before the finishing line taking very little jumping, but the casualty rate is still relatively high on account of so many coming to grief through tiredness in the latter stages, whilst the two downhill fences running away from the stands are unquestionably tricky.

➤ It's not unknown for horses to jink/slow on catching sight of the stable entrance on the run-in on the chase track.

UTTOXETER

➤ Left handed, sharp.

➤ Although sharp in nature, the track has a reputation for gruelling conditions during the winter, ability to see out the trip being of paramount importance.

➤ When the going is on the firm side it often pays to race prominently, especially on the chase course.

➤ Fences are not particularly stiff, with the casualty rate being lower than average, many casualties occurring as a result of fatigue in the latter stages.

➤ Ten hurdles (instead of the usual eight) jumped over two miles, placing an increased emphasis on jumping.

WARWICK

➤ Left handed, and flat with the exception of a fairly steep climb soon after the winning line which descends in gradual fashion to the turn into the back straight.

➤ Essentially a sharp track by virtue of the tight bends, notwithstanding a long back straight.

➤ Widely regarded as a tricky jumping track on account of five fences coming in quick succession in the back straight, but the casualty rate is one of the lowest in the country.

➤ Front runners/those ridden prominently tend to do well over both hurdles and fences.

WETHERBY

➤ Left handed, galloping.

➤ Nine fences to a circuit again now, though the four in the home straight have been switched to the inside of the hurdles track after problems caused by the realignment of the nearby A1; the early signs are the fences still punish those who aren't accurate.

➤ It's a very fair test for any horse but is ideal for the free-running, long-striding sort.

WINCANTON

➤ Right handed, flat and essentially sharp in character.

➤ One of the sharpest tests in the country when the ground is firmer than good, hold-up tactics invariably counter-productive.

➤ Conversely, front runners can often overdo things when the ground is testing.

➤ The fences are stiff and claim plenty of casualties, with the three in the home straight coming so close together that it often proves difficult to come from behind.

WORCESTER

➤ Flat, left-handed with easy turns.

➤ Portable fences don't take a huge amount of jumping, though many show a tendency to go right in the home straight. The casualty rate is slightly below the UK average over the past eight seasons.

➤ Long home straight should, in theory, give hold-up horses plenty of time to recover ground, but when conditions ride quick in summer months it pays more often than not to race handily.

➤ Beware betting on close finishes as camera is situated some way short of winning line.

INDEX

H

I

J

K

L

M

N

O

P

Q

R

S

INDEX

INDEX TO PHOTOGRAGHS